To: Jessie

Freedom isn't Free!

SEAL OF GOD

# SEAL OF GOD

**THE PATH IS NARROW . . . BUT THE REWARD IS GREAT**

## CHAD WILLIAMS
### with DAVID THOMAS

*Tyndale House Publishers, Inc.*
*Carol Stream, Illinois*

Visit Tyndale online at www.tyndale.com.

*TYNDALE* and Tyndale's quill logo are registered trademarks of Tyndale House Publishers, Inc.

*SEAL of God*

Designed by Ron Kaufmann

Edited by Anne Christian Buchanan

**Some of the names in this book have been changed out of respect for the privacy of the individuals mentioned.**

Library of Congress Cataloging-in-Publication Data

Williams, Chad.
   SEAL of God / Chad Williams with David Thomas.
      p. cm.
   Includes bibliographical references.
   ISBN 978-1-4143-6874-0 (sc)
1. Williams, Chad. 2. United States. Navy. SEALs—Biography. 3. Christians—United States—Biography. I. Thomas, David, date. II. Title.
   VG87.W55 2012
   359.0092—dc23
   [B]                                                                                      2011052928

Printed in the United States of America

21   20   19   18   17   16   15
15   14   13   12   11   10   9

*In loving memory of Scott Helvenston:*
*hero, mentor, and close friend.*

# CONTENTS

★   ★   ★

# ACKNOWLEDGMENTS

I HAVE THE deepest gratitude for my wife, Aubrey, who has been my motivator since the day I wrote her name on my Hell Week hat in SEAL training. She has also been my gracious sounding board, supplying much patience and beneficial judgment to the thoughts that go through my head.

A special thanks to Ray Comfort, who ignited the fuse that led to writing this book as we prayed about it together on the shoreline of Caesarea, Israel.

Thanks to my father and mother, Mark and Gina Williams, for their selfless character and actions as they dropped everything to help review and provide suggestions for each chapter of this book.

Thank you to my sister, Melissa Williams Netherton, and my mother-in-law, Nancy O'Boyle, for taking a good deal of their time to provide invaluable help and advice.

Special thanks to David Thomas, a master weaver who pulled together the threads of my story, and to Carol Traver, for giving me the opportunity to make this book happen, sharpening the edge of every chapter down to the last jot and tittle.

*Greater love has no one than this, than to lay down one's life for his friends.*

JOHN 15:13, NKJV

*Anyone who belongs to Christ has become a new person. The old life is gone; a new life has begun!*

2 CORINTHIANS 5:17

# FOREWORD

GOD SHAPES HIS MEN with the hammer of adversity and the chisel of discipline.

Here's the story of a rowdy young man who, though raised with Christian values, failed to turn them into virtues until he found himself locked in the vise of God's love.

When Chad Williams realized his dream of becoming a Navy SEAL—one of the toughest accomplishments in the military—what he had thought would bring fulfillment offered only greater emptiness. Then one day he heard a message from the Bible about another military man, a man not unlike Chad, whose life was radically transformed by God. His story is now Chad's story, as both of them found that the greatest achievement in life is to discover what we were created for.

You will be riveted by Chad's amazing story, from his trouble-filled days as a competitive skateboarder in the beach city where he was raised to the front lines of combat as a US

Navy SEAL. It's my hope that this book will inspire readers to find God's purpose for their lives too!

*Greg Laurie, senior pastor*
*Harvest Christian Fellowship*
*Riverside, California*

# CHAPTER I

# THINKING BIG

*We can make our plans, but the L*ORD *determines our steps.*

**PROVERBS 16:9**

★   ★   ★

"**I WANT TO** become a Navy SEAL."

Dad didn't say anything immediately, but his facial expression did.

*Are you really serious?*

This was the most important conversation I had ever had with my dad. We talked for forty-five minutes, perhaps an hour, with me sitting on my parents' bed and him sitting at his desk next to me. It felt like we talked forever.

The more we talked, the more Dad could see how serious I was.

Dad is the studious type. He considers all the options, then makes well-thought-out, informed decisions.

1

I definitely didn't inherit that trait from him.

Dad wanted me to spend another year in college and take more time to think about what I wanted to be when I grew up. He pointed out the reasons why he believed I was rushing into my decision:

"You didn't stick with baseball."

"You didn't stick with skateboarding."

"You didn't stick with sport fishing."

"You're not good with authority—and you want to go into the military?"

I didn't tell Dad that I had known I wanted to become a SEAL for all of a few days now. Or that I had reached my decision while spinning my truck in 360s across an empty parking lot at my college, where I had started the morning by drinking and smoking marijuana. Or that after I decided that morning to become a SEAL, I had skipped all my classes. Again.

That conversation with Dad ended like most conversations with my parents—on my terms. I marched out of the bedroom and down the hallway, dismayed once more that I wasn't being trusted. That my judgment was being doubted. That *I* was being doubted.

I didn't need anyone else to doubt me, because I was already doubting myself.

I was beginning to feel like a loser. The money I had made from sport fishing and filming skateboard commercials was running out. I was making bad grades, and I was sick of college. I was quickly becoming just another guy fresh out of high school who drank, smoked weed, and went surfing. Once the popular, thrill-seeking life of every party, I now feared I wouldn't amount to anything.

I needed to do something big. And nothing sounded bigger than becoming a Navy SEAL.

I'd considered becoming an Alaskan crab fisherman or a coal miner because I had heard those were two of the world's most dangerous occupations. But the SEALs sounded far more interesting. They shot exotic weapons; they were demolitions experts. They jumped out of airplanes into combat, and they conducted covert underwater operations.

SEa, Air, and Land. That's why they were called SEALs. They did it all, and they did it everywhere.

My mind was made up. And all my life, when I had set a goal in my mind, nothing and no one could stop me.

I had, however, developed a habit of stopping myself.

## ALL OR NOTHING

My dad was right that I hadn't stuck with baseball, skateboarding, or sport fishing. In my mind, though, I hadn't quit or given up on any of those. Instead, I reasoned with myself, I had simply grown tired of them and had moved on to the next thrill.

I was always a competitive kid, and baseball was my first sport. I started playing in T-ball leagues and made the all-star teams as I progressed through the different age levels. I pitched and played shortstop, and every day after my dad got off work, he and I would jump the fence to a schoolyard behind our house. Until the sun went down, I would pitch to Dad, and he would hit me ground balls. Or he would pitch to me so I could practice my batting.

When my brother, Todd, became old enough, he joined us too. It's a good thing Todd was two years younger than me, because he turned out to be extremely talented. Despite the age difference, he was right behind me talentwise, pushing me. Except being the best wasn't as important to Todd as it was to me. Winning or losing didn't make or break his day. The best way to describe the difference between us in sports is that Todd loved to win and I hated to lose.

I tried out for our high school baseball team as a freshman. I did well during the tryouts but didn't make the roster. "You're just not big enough for the team," the coach told me. I weighed only ninety-nine pounds at the time.

The next year the coach remembered my tryout and offered me a spot on the team. I declined. By that point I had moved full bore into skateboarding.

For a while, I had been torn between baseball and skateboarding and had a difficult time deciding which I wanted to spend more time doing. An unexpected meeting helped make my decision.

One day I was doing some skateboarding tricks at Seal Beach, less than ten miles up the Pacific Coast Highway from our home in Huntington Beach, California. Beatle Rosecrans, a big name in skateboarding, was in the area for a professional competition. He saw some of my tricks and came over to introduce himself. That meeting and my skill level eventually led to a sponsorship from the sports equipment company Vans that kept me in free shoes, clothes, and skateboard equipment for the next few years.

Baseball was officially in the rearview mirror and fading.

The Vans sponsorship boosted my popularity. I had their newest shoes before anyone else at school could purchase them in stores, and mine came free. I wasn't just a part of the in-crowd. The in-crowd hung out around *me*.

As my skateboarding progressed, I became a professional amateur of sorts. In addition to the goodies from Vans, I got to take a couple of all-expenses-paid, out-of-state trips with an extreme sports team, performing choreographed routines with in-line skaters and bikers. That was a blast. We would show off our tricks on half-pipe ramps and tabletop launch ramps while music pulsated in the background.

I remember one really cool stunt. One of the bikers would tow me up a ramp. I would launch into the air. Then another biker would be launched over me while he performed a backflip.

The crowds ate up our shows, and I ate up their attention. I was the team's only teenager—not yet old enough to own a driver's license, but traveling across the country with a group of high-level extreme athletes in their twenties and thirties. It was exciting to be the young gun on the team.

Skateboarding also led me into television commercials. I made eight different commercials, performing with a skateboard in all of them.

One was a SONIC commercial in which I skateboarded

past an elderly man and startled him. "Hey, you little hotdogger!" he yelled at me, and then a carhop delivered a SONIC hot dog to him.

I even had lines in a couple of commercials—like the one for Go-GURT, a yogurt product from Yoplait that squeezed out of a tube. For that shoot, I did a few tricks while a young boy watched in awe. He was eating yogurt from a cup, and I was skateboarding with my tube of Go-GURT. I grabbed an extra tube, tossed it to him, and said my line. "Hey," I told the boy, "lose the spoon."

Another speaking commercial pushed Nestlé's new Itzakadoozie frozen treats. I was about fifteen or sixteen at the time, but I was small for my age and looked younger. So I played someone about eleven or twelve alongside a girl about that age. Through trick photography, we looked like we were skating on the frozen snacks. "What is it?" we both asked as a close-up of the treats was shown. "Itzakadoozie!"

I handled those easy lines well enough, but it was my skateboarding skills that had brought the opportunity to be in the commercials. I made good money, too, which was put aside for me until I turned eighteen. Then it helped me buy a brand-new black 2002 Toyota Tundra pickup with big wheels, aftermarket rims, and a suspension lift. That certainly didn't diminish my popularity.

The ability to do the commercials was a definite perk in those days, but it was the skateboarding itself that I lived for. Competitive skateboarding is the proper name for the sport because it's as much about one-upmanship as anything else.

**CHAD WILLIAMS**

When a competitor broke out a new trick, I felt like I not only had to learn his trick and perform it better, but also come up with an original trick of my own that topped his.

It takes countless hours on a board to develop the high level of muscle memory needed to perform the best tricks, and I had the will to consistently put in the hours. I would practice in the morning before school, then as soon as I returned home from school I would grab my board and practice until nine or ten o'clock, continuing under the streetlights after the sun went down.

There is a reason I didn't include homework in that schedule: I didn't do my homework.

## TOO COOL FOR SCHOOL

My disdain for losing a skateboarding competition definitely contributed to my poor performance in school, but it wasn't the main reason. Truth was, I strongly disliked academic work and did everything I could to avoid it.

I prided myself on being able to write a complete book report without actually reading the book. I would skim the first sentence of each paragraph because I hated reading. When I didn't feel like skimming, I would cheat. I googled my way through my share of book reports.

Somehow I passed most of my classes—barely. I made mostly Cs and Ds, and that was good enough for me.

One time on a placement exam—one of those Scantron tests where you pencil in the answer bubbles for multiple-choice questions—I went through and randomly filled in circles. I didn't read a single question on the test. I don't know what my score was on that one, but it was poor enough to have me placed into a special development class for students who needed extra help learning how to read. Of course, I could read just fine and didn't belong in that class, but I didn't care.

Part of the learning process was for class members to read aloud. We did it "popcorn style." One student would read aloud until the teacher said, "Enough. Popcorn someone else." That student would point to another student, who would pick up the reading at that point. When the assigned reading was completed, we were given free time for the rest of class.

I was a popular popcorn target because I was good at reading aloud. A student would popcorn me, and I would read as fast as I could until the teacher stopped me, then I'd popcorn someone else. He or she would read for a while, then when our teacher said to stop, I'd get picked to read again. To add some life into the boring texts, I read my parts in different voices. The other students cracked up every time.

Finally, after about a month or so, I was moved out of the special development class. But it was a fun month, and it provided me an opportunity to become popular with a different crowd. And in those days I really craved being the center of attention—no matter what it took.

I'm sure the kids who weren't in my circle of friends didn't think too much of me, though. I could be mean to kids in what I considered a "lesser" group. For instance, I thought nothing of throwing a slice of pizza at someone in the school cafeteria. It was an effective way to draw laughs.

I never started fights or anything like that. Remember, I was small for my age. But I had big friends, and I was a big talker. I knew that, if need be, my buddies could finish with their size what I could start with my mouth. We never wound up in anything more than a harmless high school tiff, but I look back now and wonder how I could have been such a jerk.

Most of the problems I caused in school were what you might call disruptive behavior. I knew well the routes from my classrooms to the principal's office. Mostly, I would get sent there for cutting up in class too much.

My junior year at Marina High School in Huntington Beach, the principal warned my parents that I was down to my last chance. One more foul-up, he said, and I would be booted from the school.

Maybe my parents were fed up. Or maybe they didn't think I could keep a clean record the rest of the school year. Whatever the reason, they decided to take me out of Marina and put me into a Christian school—Calvary Chapel Costa Mesa. My parents were Christians, and I guess they hoped that a Christian school would help straighten me out.

It didn't.

I was a poor fit at Calvary Chapel High School because I felt different from the rest of the students. I did like the fact that they had a surfing team. I enjoyed surfing, although skateboarding was still my main sport. Skateboarding, with the commercials and freebies from Vans, is what made me popular and gave me my identity.

Most of my time at Calvary Chapel was spent trying to get kicked out so I could rejoin my friends at Marina. I acted up in class, disrespected my teachers, and didn't do my homework. I constantly hounded my parents, too, telling them I didn't want to attend that school.

"You guys shouldn't have taken me out of Marina. That's where my friends are," I would say, trying to put a guilt trip on them. "How could you do this to me?"

The final semester of my senior year, my parents relented and said they would take me out of the Christian school.

*Yes!* I thought when they told me. *I pulled that one off.* (Calvary Chapel teachers probably celebrated as much as I did.)

My grand plan hit a snag, though. My old high school wouldn't take me back. So my parents enrolled me in Huntington Beach High, and I finished out my final semester there. I didn't get to graduate with my friends, but at least I was out of Calvary Chapel.

I did make one decision during my final semester of high school that turned out for good, though. On a trip to Disneyland with a couple of friends, we snuck into the park for free through a secret location. Once we were in the park, my friends and I took a seat on a ledge to begin planning out the time we had left. At that moment I noticed a girl who caught my eye like no one else ever had. I watched intently as she got in line with a friend to ride Space Mountain.

Without saying anything to my two buddies, I jumped to my feet and ran as fast as I could to get in line immediately behind her. The wait for the ride was about an hour. I figured that would give me plenty of time to work up the courage to talk to this girl, who I was basically stalking.

Her name was Aubrey. She was three years younger than I was. And let me tell you, it was love at first sight! As it turned out, she lived in Huntington Beach too. We spent the rest of the evening together at the park, and I still remember the spot where I made my first move to hold her hand. After exchanging phone numbers, we parted ways, but I knew it wouldn't be the last time I saw her. There was something special about this girl.

I was right. The next thing I knew, I was asking her something I had never asked anyone before: "Will you be my girlfriend?"

## GONE FISHING

Periodically throughout my high school years, I worked as a deckhand on sport-fishing boats and continued to do so into my first year of college. I would go out on multiple-day trips, fishing for albacore, bluefin, and yellowfin tuna. My parents would drop me off at the boat on Friday night, our crew would head out onto the Pacific Ocean, we'd fish all weekend, and my parents would pick me up Monday morning back at the harbor. Our boat would dock around five in the morning, and I would be on my way to school by seven thirty. Sometimes I still smelled like fish when I walked into school.

To spend three nights out on a fishing boat at that age was exciting. It wasn't anything near as challenging as what you might see today on the Discovery Channel show *Deadliest Catch*, which chronicles the lives of Alaskan crab fishermen, but there were definitely some similarities. For instance, we would sleep only two or three hours per night. Looking back, I can see that learning to deal with sleep deprivation on those fishing boats helped me in my SEAL training later.

During summertime, when I wasn't in school, I spent even more time on the fishing boats. Sometimes we would take fifteen-day trips, come home for a day off, then set out for another fifteen days of fishing.

There was certainly no slacking off on a boat. I was expected to give 110 percent for an entire trip. As a deck-hand, if I didn't keep up with the veteran fishermen's tempo, they'd let me know about it in some pretty salty terms. It had to be that way because some boats had a two-ton fish hole to fill. There was no room on a boat for someone who worked at less than maximum effort.

The work was hard, the hours were long—again, good training for the SEALs—and the pay was great, which may not have been a good thing. I could make five hundred dollars or more in a twenty-four-hour period. Some trips, I came home with two thousand dollars in cash. That's a ton of spending money for a teenager, and it would later cause me problems.

## RAISING CAIN

I cannot imagine what my parents must have thought as they read or heard Proverbs 22:6:

*Direct your children onto the right path,*
*and when they are older, they will not leave it.*

Mom and Dad directed me onto the right path, but I didn't follow it. They must have wondered if I would ever find my way back onto that path before making a major mistake from which I couldn't recover.

As the wild and rebellious child of our family, I put my parents through more stress and worry than they should have experienced.

My dad, Mark, grew up near Compton in southern Los Angeles County. It was a rough neighborhood. He has told me about how at his school the students had to run to the buses while teachers stood outside to protect them from neighborhood gangs. Because of the violence, Dad's parents moved their family down the coast a little to Huntington Beach, where he attended Marina High and met my mom, Gina. They married soon after graduating from high school.

Dad has been an appraiser for all my life, and his job often allowed him to work from home. That made it easier to get an early start on our baseball practices at the school behind our house. Dad was a good athlete, and my brother and I picked up our love of sports and our athletic abilities from him.

Dad stayed in good shape, and I learned what it meant to work out by watching him. When he pitched to us for batting practice, we would go through a bucket of about fifty baseballs. After we had hit the balls all over the schoolyard, Dad would run around picking up the balls as part of his workout.

There was one particular time when Dad considered becoming a fireman and was trying to get in shape for that. My brother and I would tag along with him, and with a son's wonder I would watch him execute something like twenty-five pull-ups. Even as a lightweight kid, I could only do about ten. I wanted to be able to do pull-ups like Dad. We would go for runs, and it seemed like Dad could run forever. He could also swim fifty laps in our swimming pool.

My dad amazed me with his athletic ability. He's still in great shape, and when I introduce him to my friends, they say he looks way too young to be my dad.

"Yeah, he's my dad," I proudly tell them.

My mom, bless her heart, sure suffered a lot of undue stress when I was growing up. Mom has always been a sweetheart. She modeled for me how to show compassion toward others and how to forgive without holding a grudge. In my younger days, I didn't put into practice much of what I observed from her. But when I became a Christian at age twenty-three and experienced a dramatic and complete turnaround in my life, those traits began to shine through. I know exactly who I picked them up from.

I have a sister named Melissa who is three-and-a-half years

older than me. She always made straight As—she started reading at age two—and competed in beauty pageants at a young age. The trophies she amassed are still in my parents' garage. I've already talked about Todd, who is two years younger than I am. The baby of the family is my sister Allison, who is four years younger than me.

As the two boys of the family, Todd and I grew up doing just about everything together. As the older brother, I could almost always persuade Todd to take part in mischief with me. But Todd had one dangerous weakness: he had a conscience.

I had no problem with not telling my parents the things we were doing. Todd, on the other hand, thought they needed to know everything, even things he knew they would disapprove of.

Such as the time we tied dog bones to Allison.

Our little sister was always really quiet and would follow Todd and me around and watch everything we did. She really looked up to us, and we took full advantage. We could convince her to do anything.

Our family had a German shepherd named Haas that Todd and I liked to pretend was our police dog. One day Allison, who was about six at the time, was wearing a pair of overalls that had a lot of pockets. That gave me an idea I shared with Todd: "Let's stuff as many dog bones as we can into Allison's pockets and sic Haas on her."

"I don't think that's such a good idea," said the Williams boy with the conscience.

"Shut up," I ordered him. "We're gonna do it."

Of course, sweet little Allison let us load her up with bones. Then we told her to run around the yard, and we turned our police dog loose. Haas kept chasing her and going after every bone he could. In the process, Haas bit Allison's arm. She had to go to the emergency room to get a couple of staples to close the bite mark.

That time, I actually was able to convince Todd to suppress his good conscience. Our parents didn't find out we were to blame for the dog's behavior until months later.

Another time, Todd was pitching baseballs to me, and I hit him in the stomach with a line drive on purpose. Todd wanted to run home to tell Mom and Dad, but I wouldn't let him. I grabbed him and decided I would hold him down on the ground until his stomach quit hurting and there wouldn't be any reason to tell. Todd did everything he could to get out from under me, but I was stronger. I didn't let him get up until he was pain free and no longer inclined to tell.

Todd and I did a lot of things that could potentially get us into trouble at home. When I was with my friends, though, we did things that could have gotten us into trouble with the law. Some of them were pretty stupid. Unfortunately, most of them were my ideas.

We liked to hide and throw rocks at cars, for instance. If the driver stopped to chase us, that made it more fun. Or we would take two trash cans and tie them together with a long rope. We would lay the rope across a street and keep the trash cans on opposite sides of the street. Just as a car drove by, we would tighten the rope so that it caught onto the bumper, and the car would drag the trash cans down the street. We would take off running, laughing hard. When we finally stopped, we would laugh some more as we described for each other what we saw of the driver's reaction.

Another stunt we would pull off was to climb to the roof of the school behind our house. We even found a way to get into the school from the roof. We especially got a kick out of hauling old bicycles onto the roof. We would ride the bike full speed, jump off just as we got to the edge of the roof, and watch the bike fall twenty feet to the ground.

Occasionally someone in the neighborhood would see us on the roof and call the police. But we had spent so much time up there that we had escape routes mapped out in our minds. We knew where to hide and how to get down before the police caught us.

I brought Todd along for some of these shenanigans. When he was with us, I was more concerned about his telling Mom or Dad than I was about getting caught by the cops.

"I don't think we should be doing this," Todd would say.

"You better not tell Mom and Dad, or else . . ."

Then we would do it.

## PLAYING WITH FIRE

Me and Todd—I know that "Todd and I" is proper grammar, but I really should put my name first because I was the one dragging him into these situations—were especially fascinated with fires and explosions. We would gather cardboard and papers, take them over to the schoolyard, and set them ablaze. I don't know why, but watching things burn entertained us.

On the few occasions when we heard a police helicopter approaching, the game was on. We would run to hide under a tree, then watch the helicopter until we were in a blind spot. Then we would run undetected to another tree. We would run from tree to tree like that until we were safely away from the school.

One of the ways Todd and I made money as kids was to buy candy from a man who sold it on the local streets, then take it to school and sell it. We didn't make much profit off each sale, but we were good at saving what we did make. When we had saved up enough, we would go to a store and buy model-rocket engines, telling the store owner that our dad had a model rocket and the equipment.

We would take the engines home and gut them with a screwdriver to get the black powder from inside. Then we'd wrap the powder up tight in a toilet paper roll, light the roll, and run. The toilet paper roll would blow up into small pieces.

Naturally, being the competitive person that I am, I reached the point of needing to make a larger and louder explosion. I was around twelve or thirteen by then, and I enlisted my friend Matt for the experiment.

We saved up for fifteen model-rocket engines. We were going to go big this time! Instead of using a toilet paper roll, we used the cardboard tube from a paper towel roll. We stuffed the tube with powder and capped each end with surfboard wax. Then we took a needle and thread and ran the thread through the tube, in one end and out the other. We did this several times, running multiple threads through the tube. Then we took a can of spray-on deodorant and sprayed the thread to make it more flammable. That was our wick.

We took our homemade explosive over to the school behind my house and lit it. The wick was working great, burning down, burning down, burning down . . .

We knew this explosion was going to be so big and blow so much debris that we didn't even plan to watch. Content merely to *hear* this one, we found a safe spot around a corner of the school building and waited for the big boom.

We waited ten seconds. Fifteen seconds. But no boom. Nothing was happening.

Matt and I looked at each other as if to ask which of us was going to check on the wick. Naturally, I was the one.

I walked up to the tube and leaned my head over to take an up close look. I saw a tiny red ember. I had just enough time to raise one arm in front of my face.

*Boom!*

Unfortunately, it was as big an explosion as we had hoped for.

My right forearm, my right hand, and parts of my face were burning. I couldn't hear anything but continual ringing in my ears. I could tell Matt was yelling something, but I didn't know what. He was looking at me as though he saw a ghost.

We immediately ran to a drinking fountain and splashed

whatever water we could onto my burns. I was in pain by that point. We ran to Matt's house, where I jumped into his shower, clothes still on, and turned on cold water.

Matt was freaking out. "What are we gonna do? What are we gonna do?" he kept saying when he wasn't asking if I was okay.

We knew we weren't going to be able to get away with this one.

"Can you please say you were by yourself when this happened?" Matt asked. "What are you going to tell your parents?"

I hadn't figured that out yet, so we both started praying.

*Please, God, make everything be okay. If you help us this time, if you get us out of this one, we'll never do anything like this again.*

I went home. My mom wasn't home, and my dad was busy at one end of the house, so I was able to sneak in. I grabbed my pillow, jumped into the shower with it, and got the pillow wet with cold water to try to stop, or at least ease, the burning. I felt horrible.

"Oh, God, please help me, please help me," I kept praying.

My brother overheard me. Being the kid with a conscience, he told my dad something was wrong with me.

I was on my bed, lying facedown on my wet pillow, when Dad knocked on the door.

*I'm not going to be able to hide this*, I told myself.

"Chad?" Dad said. "You okay?"

"I'm all right."

"Are you sure?"

"Yeah."

"Can I come in?"

"No."

Dad came into my room anyway.

*I'm done with this*, I thought.

When we had first reached Matt's house, I had looked like a chimney sweep at the end of a long job—covered with so much black powder that my burns weren't visible. But now my face was cleaned up and bright red like a shiny apple.

"A rocket went off, and I got a little burned," I told Dad, though obviously that was a wild understatement.

Dad took me to the emergency room. I had suffered second-degree burns.

It took awhile for my mom to get the message that I had gotten hurt. By the time she made it to the emergency room, Dad and I were back in the car and preparing to leave. I'll never forget seeing my mom's face as she looked at me from her vehicle next to ours. I knew it looked bad. It *was* bad. Her Chevrolet Astro minivan was weaving in the lane behind us as we drove home. I was worried about her.

My parents got into an argument that night.

"You were supposed to be watching him!" Mom accused my dad.

"He told me he was just going skateboarding," Dad countered.

I *had* told Dad that. And I felt awful about what I had done and what I had caused. I knew it was all my fault.

I ended up having to visit a plastic surgeon, and he said my burns would require skin grafting. That's when I realized just how serious the situation was.

*I might not ever look the same again*, I feared.

One thing I still clearly remember is how often my parents prayed for me during that time. I would wake up in the middle of the night, walk through the house, and hear them saying my name in prayer. It actually frightened me a little that they were praying for me so much.

Our church was praying too—the entire church—Mom and Dad told me.

We went back to the plastic surgeon several days later.

"Wait a minute," the surgeon said. "How long has this been? This is the same kid that was here the other day?"

The surgeon told my parents that it looked like I had already made several weeks of progress and I might not need a skin graft after all.

I did totally lose pigment in some areas of my skin, and I had to avoid overexposure to sunlight for a few months. But I never had to have that skin graft, and today you would have to look very, very closely at my arm to see the reminders of that paper towel roll with the slow fuse.

## WRONG PERSPECTIVE

The rocket incident perfectly represents my growing-up years: make a stupid decision, get myself into trouble, say a quick prayer, then watch everything somehow turn out just fine.

Our family started going to church when I was six or

seven. We weren't regular attendees at first, but we did go. Over the next few years, I noticed my parents' faith increasing. So did our attendance at church—much to my annoyance.

I didn't like church. It felt like school to me, and I didn't want to go.

A few times, when the six of us were getting ready to leave for church, I sneaked out of the house and hid down the block. I knew my parents had to leave by a certain time to get to church on time and that they couldn't spend too long looking for me. After they left, I had the morning to myself.

Even when my parents did get me to church, I found ways to get out of Sunday school class—like asking the teacher if I could go to the bathroom. Then I would sneak out to the parking lot, get my skateboard out of the back of our Suburban—which I had made sure was unlocked when everyone stepped out—and ride around until Sunday school was over.

It wasn't that I didn't believe in God. But I thought he was just someone to pray to when I was in trouble and couldn't fix things by myself. I knew Jesus was important, but I didn't understand the Cross. I had no knowledge of the basics of Christianity. I couldn't even quote John 3:16 like everyone else seemingly could. (Ditching Sunday school didn't help with my spiritual ignorance, of course.)

I knew I was living in a way that was displeasing to God, but I saw no real need to change. I actually believed that knowing I wasn't living like he wanted me to made me better off than everyone else like me. *Hey*, I would reason, *at least*

*I know I'm not doing right. That has to count for something with God.*

Basically, I believed that all I had to do was say "sorry" right before I died, and I would be on my way to heaven.

Looking back on those days, all I can do is shake my head.

# CHAPTER 2

# DECISIONS, DECISIONS

*Though they stumble, they will never fall,*
*for the LORD holds them by the hand.*

PSALM 37:24

★　★　★

**MY REBELLIOUS NATURE** led me to drinking alcohol, but not right away. I resisted peer pressure for a long time, mainly because I was so into my sports and I didn't want to jeopardize my performance. But when my family moved, I decided it was time for me to have my first drink.

It was a stupid reason to experiment. We were moving only a few miles, to a different house in Huntington Beach. But we were leaving the home I had grown up in, and all my memories were from that house. That seemed at the time like a good enough excuse to be angry. When I saw my old bedroom empty during our move, I determined that drinking alcohol for the first time could be my way of getting back at my parents for making me move. The fact that it was illegal for a seventeen-year-old to drink didn't bother me a bit.

Kevin, a friend from the neighborhood we were leaving, had been pestering me to drink with him for a long time, so he welcomed my decision. He had some Bacardi rum—one of those big bottles with a filter on the end to keep the rum from coming out too fast. We took the bottle out beside his house.

"Just chug it," he told me. "Don't try to taste it. Just drink as much as you can." So I did.

It wasn't a problem for me to chug it. I didn't gag or choke or anything like that. Kevin actually had to tell me to stop chugging. He grabbed the bottle and took a drink. Then I chugged some more. I felt a sort of buzz coming on, and I liked that feeling.

Kevin and I left for a party, and I remember laughing harder than I had ever laughed in my life. I felt great the entire night. To my surprise, the next morning I didn't have a hangover. In fact, I felt pretty good.

*That wasn't so bad*, I thought.

Looking back now, I wish I had gotten as sick as a dog. I wish I had thrown up all night and been suffering from a headache so bad the next morning that I couldn't open my eyes in a room with the lights on. That might have saved me a lot of trouble later on. But I never felt the aftereffects most people experience from a night of drinking.

Only days after my first drink, Kevin also introduced me to marijuana.

Again, we were at his home. He took me into his garage, where he had a bong already filled with smoke. He was "milking," or preparing, the marijuana. I inhaled the smoke and stepped back. I inhaled again. And again. I kept taking hits. But I wasn't feeling any different.

Kevin was already getting high.

"You're not feeling anything?" he asked.

"Nope."

Kevin shook his head in disbelief.

"All right," he said, "we'll keep going."

So we did.

I took a hit. Nothing. Another hit. Nothing.

Then it hit me—hard. I instantly went from feeling nothing to thinking I might be killing myself.

"I think I'm dying," I kept telling Kevin.

In addition to tripping out from the weed, Kevin was now freaking out about me.

"Kevin, I think I'm dying," I said again.

This went on for maybe ten or fifteen minutes, with Kevin asking if I was okay and me continuing to say I thought I was dying. We were close to calling 911 when I started to come down a little bit. I gradually got better, and with the scare over, we headed out for the night.

We took our skateboards and rode around the streets, parks, and schoolyards. Kevin fell off his board, and the board rolled into the street, where a red Corvette ran over it.

We just looked at each other as though to say, "This is the weirdest night ever."

But as with the first time I drank alcohol, I felt good and enjoyed myself.

As time went by, I drank and smoked more. I never actually bought marijuana. I mostly just smoked it when friends had some they wanted to smoke together—maybe once a week. But I did spend my money on alcohol. I had plenty of money from my sport-fishing job to keep myself and my friends well stocked. No, I wasn't old enough to purchase it legally, but when you're providing the funding, it's easy to find someone willing to make the purchase for you.

I didn't get into extremely heavy drinking before finishing high school, but alcohol was definitely part of my life. And drunk or not, I was an idiot behind the wheel.

After a graduation party, I remember driving friends around in my new truck at three in the morning. I had the cab filled with my friends, plus five or six in the bed of the truck. I topped out at more than one hundred miles per hour while playing Russian road roulette, running through red lights. That scared my friends, especially the ones in back.

"Stop it, Chad! Let us out!" they yelled at me.

I looked at them like they were sissies. I was having fun on my thrill ride and couldn't understand why they weren't too.

I drove like that several times and never got caught. I felt invincible, and every time I drove like a madman and got away with it, that feeling of invincibility increased. I never thought about my friends' safety because there was never a sense that anything would happen—or could happen—when I was driving.

## MORE PARTIES THAN CLASSES

After making it through high school, I enrolled at Golden West College, a community college in Huntington Beach.

Even though I had hated high school, going to college seemed like the natural thing to do. That's what most of my friends were doing, and that was the next step in the path I was supposed to take.

Except I took college about as seriously as I took high school.

I had a friend named Mike who shared my aversion to school—and my love of surfing. Some days, we would meet up before class and buy a package of SweeTarts candy from a vending machine. We would take a SweeTart and flip it like a coin. If we caught it with the "SweeTarts" side up, that was our signal to skip class and go surfing. If we didn't get the "SweeTarts" on the first flip, we would go best two out of three—or three out of five, if we needed to. I recall one time going to best of nine before receiving permission from the candy to head to the beach.

With that type of attitude, I don't have to tell you that I wasn't making the dean's list. One of my classes was a film class in which all we had to do was watch movies and make small presentations describing what the movies were about.

I made a D.

My alcohol and marijuana consumption increased during

my first semester in college, especially the alcohol. I was drinking just about every day by that point. I felt good when I drank and still wasn't suffering hangovers. And I was partying a lot—something I hadn't really done in high school.

My friends and I were still underage at that point, so we had to sneak into clubs. One friend, Jammel, and I would go to one club in particular and sometimes wait an hour or even two for the right moment to sneak in. We would sit in my truck and watch the security guard, identifying the pattern of how he turned his back or looked away. We would time it perfectly to where we could slip in right behind the guard.

Sometimes only one of us would get in, and the other would have to wait for another opportunity to try again. For some reason, Jammel usually made it in ahead of me. Because he looked older than his age, he could then distract the security guard by asking a question or pretending he was looking for something he had dropped on the ground. While the guard was listening to Jammel, I'd make my move.

Once inside, we always remained nervous about getting caught. We were afraid to order alcohol—Jammel looked like he could be old enough, but I still looked like a fifteen-year-old—so we would drink before we went to the bar. Sometimes we met people inside who would order for us.

It was on a night out with Jammel and other friends that I thought I might finally get caught doing something stupid.

It was about three o'clock in the morning when we left our favorite club after a night of drinking, and I was driving Jammel home at my usual high speed. We came to the top of a hill with a long downward slope. The area was well lit, and I could see that the shopping center down the hill on the left was empty, so I didn't slow down. We came to a red light at the entrance to the shopping center's large parking lot, and I raced right through it, probably going more than one hundred miles per hour.

Then I discovered the parking lot wasn't empty after all.

The police officer hiding there hit his lights, caught up to me as I slowed, and pulled me over.

*This is it*, I thought as the officer walked toward my truck. *I ran a red light going triple digits, I've been drinking, and there's alcohol on my breath. I am sooo toast.*

The officer looked over my driver's license.

"Have you been drinking?" he asked.

"No, sir."

He asked again. "Have you been drinking?"

"No, sir," I lied again.

"Where are you guys going?"

"I'm taking him home," I said as I pointed to Jammel. "We have just another mile to go. I could tell that nobody was going to pull out of the parking lot. I'm sorry."

"All right," the officer said. He wrote out a ticket for running the red light, but nothing else.

"I'm going to follow you guys home," he told me.

"Yes, sir," I answered.

Somehow I had gotten away with another one.

The officer followed us to Jammel's house, then pulled away. I stayed at Jammel's to sleep for what remained of the morning. Once again, I thanked God for covering for me and promised I would never do anything like that again.

Of course, those promises never lasted more than a couple of days, at most.

## OFF THE SKATEBOARD

Partying soon began to take over the time I spent skateboarding. My passion for skateboarding seemed to have burned out, just like my interest in baseball and sport fishing. The preparations for competitions had become a job that was no longer fun or exciting. So I just started doing less and less of it.

What I realized after my skateboard interest faded was just how much I was identified with skateboarding.

"This is Chad. He's a competitive skateboarder, and he's sponsored by Vans," my friends would say when they introduced me. Now when anyone introduced me—if they did introduce me—I was just Chad. That's it—Chad Williams. Just another community college student.

Friends were telling me I should get back into skateboarding, and I would watch the sport on television and see names of people I had competed against.

*I used to beat him*, I'd think. *That could be me on TV. I should have stuck with skateboarding. I could be making big money.*

But I didn't want to be skateboarding, and I didn't want to be that skateboarder on TV. I did, though, want to be *somebody*, and I was beginning to feel like a nobody.

So I threw my energy into my new identity as a wild partyer.

I would stay out partying until five in the morning sometimes. I didn't like my chances of going home, sleeping for a couple of hours, then waking up with the alarm in time for class. So I would go to the school and sleep in the hallway, leaning against the wall outside my classroom.

Early-arriving professors would see me sleeping in the hallway and ask, "Is everything okay at home, Chad?"

"Yeah, I'm fine," I'd say, then get up for class.

On occasion, I would even drink Jose Cuervo and smoke a little marijuana in the parking lot before my first class. For some reason I thought it was cool to show up to class with my eyes glazed over and a don't-care attitude.

Two-year colleges typically attract groups of older students, and the older students at my school looked at me like I was a loser. I really couldn't argue with them. I was eighteen years old and feeling like life had already passed me by, like I had blown my chance at becoming anything successful. I had no plan. All I had was a list of activities that I had poured myself into completely, then walked away from.

It was early in my second semester of college, and my life was in a state of limbo. I was miserable. I considered taking a year off from school, but to do what? I had nothing I could do. In fact, I was already doing nothing, and that was getting me nowhere. Plus, I had run through almost all the money I'd made sport fishing and filming commercials. Soon I wouldn't be able to support my party habits.

The morning remains crystal clear in my memory. I was in the school parking lot, early for my early class. Rain was pouring, and I could see the asphalt was slick and getting slicker.

I started up my truck and did 360s in the empty parking lot. I did burnouts, feeling a thrill from the sound of squealing tires grasping for traction. I laughed as both hands fought with the steering wheel to regain control of the sliding back end.

After a few minutes, I stopped and lit up a joint. While I smoked, I pondered my life.

*What am I going to do?* I asked myself. *I need to do something. But not just anything—something big. I need the attention I used to enjoy, the excitement. I've faded. I'm a nobody. I need to do something significant. But what?*

The idea of becoming a Navy SEAL had always been in the back of my mind. As a young kid, I had pretended I was a SEAL while swimming in our pool. During high school, I had loved the movie *Navy SEALs* with Charlie Sheen. I had also watched TV documentaries about SEALs that instilled in me a fascination not only with SEALs' jobs but also with their lifestyles.

On my fishing trips, some of the veterans had told stories about their experiences in Alaskan crab fishing, and I had been intrigued by the dangers and sense of adventure they described. But in my mind, not even Alaskan crab fishing or coal mining could offer the same rush as the SEALs could.

*That's it,* I decided as the aroma of freshly smoked weed wafted around the cab of my pickup.

*I'm going to become a SEAL.*

## THE WORKOUTS BEGIN

I anticipated that becoming a SEAL would be the most difficult thing I would attempt in my life, but I had no doubt I would make it. SEAL candidates vow they will die before they quit, and most wind up quitting anyway, but I just knew that wouldn't happen to me. I would for sure become a SEAL. And once I did, I would be able to sit on top of that mountain for the rest of my life. I would be happy from that point on. Making it through the Hell Week of SEAL training alone would become a milestone accomplishment in my life.

I decided right then and there that I was finished with alcohol and marijuana. I couldn't drink and smoke and reach the peak physical condition necessary to become a SEAL. I put my truck back into gear and drove across the street to a schoolyard. There was a set of monkey bars on the playground, and I did as many pull-ups as I could. Then I jumped back up and grabbed the bar and again did as many pull-ups as I could. Then I climbed on top of the monkey bars and did the same routine with dips. Then I did push-ups. Not even an hour after determining my new life plan, I was going at it 110 percent.

That was the first of what would become daily workouts for me. On the Internet I found a sixteen-week workout plan for building up to become a SEAL. I began with the eighth week. Instead of starting with the two-mile runs suggested for beginners, I launched my program by running five or six miles. I steadily built up my repetitions of pull-ups, dips, and push-ups. I would sneak into a neighborhood swimming pool and swim for one hour straight, then relax my muscles in the hot tub.

I recruited friends who were in pretty good shape to work out with me, but they couldn't keep up. Some of my workouts lasted eight hours, and I loved every minute. I was completely consumed with the idea of becoming a SEAL.

I also bought a book called *Rogue Warrior* by Richard Marcinko, and although in school I did everything possible to avoid reading, I couldn't put this one down.

Marcinko was a high school dropout who became a SEAL. He took part in the Iranian hostage rescue attempt in 1980 and the United States' invasion of Grenada. His story had me absolutely riveted. I devoured every page, imagining myself right there with the author as he exchanged gunfire in combat and climbed oil rigs in crisply executed takeovers. I loved reading about what a tight-knit group the SEALs were and how they all had special nicknames for each other. Marcinko's book affirmed that this was the big thing I wanted to do.

A few days into my extreme workouts, I decided it was time to talk to Dad.

## THE TALK

He was working from home, at the desk in my parents' bedroom, the afternoon I walked in and delivered the news.

At first he was caught off guard. As we began talking, Dad was looking me over. I could tell he was trying to gauge how serious I was about becoming a SEAL. I was as serious about this as I'd ever been about anything in my life, and I sensed he was picking up on that.

As Dad began to cite examples of other things I previously had been so serious about doing, I felt like he was doubting that I had what it took to become a SEAL. That only made me dig my heels in deeper.

Dad wanted me to take more time to think. He suggested I spend another year in school and then take it from there. But I hadn't done well in my first semester, and I had already stopped going to classes so I could work out. Despite everything my dad said to try to convince me otherwise, I knew becoming a SEAL was the path for me.

He tried to tell me that even if I went into the Navy, there was no guarantee that I would receive the opportunity to become a SEAL. I had done research and had an answer to that. Apparently there was a contract I could sign that promised I would at least get the chance to try.

But there were still no guarantees, Dad countered. Once I was in the military, everything I did would be at the military's discretion. He warned that I could enter the Navy wanting to become a SEAL and wind up spending all my service time chipping paint off a boat.

We were at a stalemate. I wasn't convincing Dad that becoming a SEAL was what I should do, and he wasn't convincing me otherwise. When I had had enough of the conversation, I got off the bed and walked out of the room with my typical "whatever" attitude.

That night I heard the dreaded words: "Chad, we need to talk to you."

Dad had told Mom, and now we were going to have the same conversation in the same room, but with Mom involved this time.

My mom cried from the start.

"You're going to kill me," she told me at one point, reminding me that I'd already taken a few years off her life with the failed paper towel roll experiment.

"I can't go through this," she said. "You could go to war and get killed. We might never see you again."

I eventually walked out on that conversation too.

The pain on my mom's face bothered me, but it didn't deter me. I knew nothing bad would happen to me. It never had before, and I certainly had created plenty of opportunities for something bad to happen.

*I will just need to gently lead my parents through this,* I reasoned. *They'll be there at graduation day, and they'll be all happy and proud. They just need to see me actually go through with this.*

I was going to become a SEAL because I knew that's what I wanted to be, and that's all there was to it.

Each day for the next few days, my dad brought up the topic. I sensed that mostly he wanted to see if I was still serious about becoming a SEAL, and each time we talked about it I did my best to convince him I was. We never talked long, mostly because I would cut the discussion short by saying I needed to go for my run or something like that.

One day, however, Dad surprised me. He told me he had made contact with a former SEAL, who had agreed to meet with me.

I was confused. Why was Dad suddenly interested in helping me learn more about becoming a SEAL?

"If you're really serious about this," he explained, "I figured you might as well have a good idea of what you're getting yourself into. So I found a former SEAL on the Internet. He's got a SEAL workout set up for you."

What I didn't know, and wouldn't find out until a few months later, was that Dad had asked this guy to put me through a workout so difficult that it would completely beat the idea of becoming a SEAL out of my mind.

# CHAPTER 3

# MY MENTOR

*As iron sharpens iron, so a friend sharpens a friend.*

**PROVERBS 27:17**

★  ★  ★

**I WASN'T READY.** I knew that. So I was dreading the workout Dad had set up for me. I had been working out only a couple of weeks. Yes, I had started at the halfway point of that sixteen-week training course, and I was quite pleased with my progress, but I would have preferred a couple of months' rather than a couple of weeks' worth of workouts before taking this test. I didn't want to embarrass myself.

I asked Dad to reschedule for a later date, but he refused.

"This is going to help you," he said. "You want to be a SEAL; you're about to find out what it's really like. Go hang out with a SEAL for the day."

All I knew about Scott Helvenston when I parked at the beach in Oceanside was that he was a former SEAL. If I had known more about him, I probably would have been even more nervous than I was.

Scott had become a SEAL at age seventeen—at the time, the youngest SEAL to make it through training. He'd set the record for fastest time through the obstacle course at the Naval Amphibious Base Coronado across the bay from San Diego. The record still stood when the obstacle course was redesigned, so his record will never be broken.

He served as a SEAL for twelve years, including a few years as an instructor, before leaving the military in 1994. After that, his SEAL background helped him achieve celebrity status. He trained Demi Moore for her role in the movie *G.I. Jane*, in which Moore played the first female to train as a SEAL. (It was a fictional role; women are not permitted to join the SEALs.) Scott made an appearance in that movie as a SEAL instructor and as a stuntman. He hung around Hollywood a little after that and later was a consultant for *Face/Off*, starring Nicolas Cage and John Travolta.

He appeared in two reality television series. *Combat Missions*, created by the producer of the *Survivor* series, featured members of various elite military groups in combat-type contests. Another show, *Man vs. Beast*, pitted humans against animals in an assortment of competitions. Scott, as the king of the Coronado obstacle course, competed with a chimpanzee in an obstacle-course race—and became the first person on that show to defeat an animal competitor. Scott also made a series of exercise videos, including one titled *Navy SEAL: Total Body Workout.*

I'm glad I did not know all that beforehand, because I already felt enough pressure trying to impress someone I believed was "only" a SEAL.

Oceanside was about a sixty-mile drive down the coast from where we lived. There was no way I was going to be late, so I left early and arrived with time to spare. As I waited inside my truck in the parking lot, I surveyed all the beachgoers, wondering if there was a SEAL among them.

I had never met a SEAL. Thank goodness for the documentaries I had watched on television; without them, I probably would have been looking for someone built like Charlie Sheen (who had played a SEAL onscreen). But then I saw Scott walking around in the parking lot. I knew it had to be him. Something in his bearing told me he was the guy I was looking for. His sleeveless shirt exposed incredibly muscular arms. This guy was obviously still in top physical condition.

*Oh, man*, I thought. *This is it.*

I was nervous before, but now I was worried. I stayed in my truck and watched him. He looked around, then he must have spotted me. He kept looking in my direction.

*He's a SEAL. He's aware of me. He knows it's me.*

It was a big parking lot, and the beach was full of people that day, yet he continued to look directly at me. Feeling there was nowhere to hide, I exited my truck and locked the door.

"You Chad?" he said loudly as he strode across the parking lot.

"You Scott?" I replied in his direction.

"Yep, I sure am, Bubba." I don't know why, but he kept calling me Bubba that day.

Scott wore sunglasses, so I couldn't read anything from his eyes. (I've learned that it's rare to see a SEAL without a pair of sunglasses.)

The one reassuring thing I noticed about Scott was that he wasn't tall. I was five feet seven and up to about 145 pounds at the time. Scott was probably five-nine, just a couple of inches taller than me. I guessed that he weighed around 175 pounds, albeit a rock-solid 175. That was a relief because it meant I would not have to get much bigger to make it as a SEAL. Yet the cut of his muscles confirmed that I had plenty of work ahead.

Scott introduced me to a friend named Seth, a former Marine and a big, big guy—super-muscular. Since leaving the Marines, Seth had decided he wanted to become a SEAL. He had been working out with Scott for about two years. We didn't say much as we walked to the beach. I felt like I was being sized up the entire time. Whether I would pass the test was anybody's guess.

## JUST GETTING WARMED UP

At the beach, Scott was all business. He immediately set up a portable pull-up bar.

"Let's get started," he said briskly. We would do three sets of twelve pull-ups each, and he would go first.

Scott completed his first set with no problem. Then the

big guy, Seth, completed his. I quickly worked through my first twelve. Then it was right back to Scott, so there was little recovery time between sets. Again, Scott whipped through his twelve. As Seth began his second set, I counted in my mind. He barely made ten. My competitive nature kicked in at the opportunity to beat the muscular ex-Marine. I completed my second set of twelve.

Scott easily made it through the third and final set of pull-ups. Seth struggled again, stopping after probably eight. My arms were tired from the first two sets, and there hadn't been but a couple of minutes of rest since my second set. But I managed all twelve, even though I struggled toward the end. I might even have been able to do a couple more pull-ups if needed, but it would have been close.

I was happy to have made it through all three sets and to have outperformed Seth. Then Scott informed me I hadn't been doing the pull-ups correctly. "You've got to go down all the way," Scott told me. Apparently I hadn't been hanging all the way down to the bottom with my arms fully extended.

It bothered me that Scott had found a flaw to criticize so soon into the workout, because I wanted everything I did in front of him to be perfect. It was almost as though that day, that workout, was going to determine whether I became a SEAL or not.

After the pull-ups, Scott said he wanted us to do some warm-up exercises.

*My arms and shoulders are tired, and we haven't even warmed up yet?*

As Scott took Seth and me through the warm-ups, I paid close attention to how he executed every one of them. These were exercises I would be required to perform in SEAL training, so this was a learning opportunity that could give me a competitive edge over the other trainees when that day came.

I remember one particular warm-up: flutter kicks. I would later learn that flutter kicks develop the muscles SEALs use most in underwater missions. They work the abdominal muscles, and that's an area of my body I hadn't spent much time developing.

I quickly learned I was going to pay for that oversight.

Flutter kicks aren't complicated. All you do is lie on your back, put your hands beneath your rear end, stretch out your legs about six inches off the ground, then "chop" your legs, alternately kicking them up and down without allowing your feet to touch the ground. They're sometimes called scissor kicks. It's an easy exercise to learn, but it sure is tough to do.

The worst part was that Scott was giving us a four-count as we did our kicks: "One . . . two . . . three . . . *one*. One . . . two . . . three . . . *two*. One . . . two . . . three . . . *three*," and so on. I would have been much happier if one time up and down with each leg counted as one complete repetition. Scott's count was going slowly, and my lower abs were on fire. I struggled to keep up the pace, but, again, I managed to make it through.

As we continued our warm-ups, I was pleased that I was still outdoing Seth. His heavier body weight was working against him. Being smaller, I had much less weight to move.

Scott clearly was flying through all the exercises with no hint of a problem. Seth was struggling to keep up. I was in between. *At least I'm not last*, I thought.

Then Scott said we were going for a run. This would be the real test.

## MESSAGE RECEIVED

"This is how it's going to work," Scott informed me. "We'll run real nice and easy for fifteen minutes or so. Then we'll let Seth lead, then you'll lead. Then we'll let Seth lead again, then you'll lead again."

We crossed the Pacific Coast Highway to a wetlands-type area where people walk and jog on narrow, beaten paths. After our breezy run to loosen up, Scott told Seth to lead the way. I easily kept up with Seth, so I started getting a little cocky.

*This ain't so bad*, I thought. *This is a piece of cake.*

After Seth had led for a while with me right behind him, Scott said, "All right, Bubba, why don't you go ahead and lead?"

When I took the lead, I decided to turn our run into a competition. I wanted to crush some souls, so I moved in front of Seth and set out on a pace that I knew he would have difficulty keeping up with. I even wanted to outrun Scott.

It wasn't long before I looked back and noticed that Seth was dropping back on the trail and Scott was staying back with him. I kept my pace. I wanted to leave Seth in the dust.

I looked back again. Seth was even farther back, but Scott was gaining on me—and gaining quickly. It was almost like a dog was chasing me. I started running as hard as I could because I didn't want Scott to catch me.

I didn't know how far we were going to run and didn't care by that point, because my goal now was to not be run down by Scott.

Then Scott passed me. I told myself that I had to keep up with him. So I started running even harder.

When Scott got about twenty feet ahead of me, he stopped dead in his tracks, turned to face me, and took one step off the narrow path.

*That's dumb of him*, I thought. *What is he doing? I'm going to run right past him.*

Scott stayed there, just off the path to my right, as I approached. Then, precisely as I was about to sprint past him, Scott thrust his right arm forward and punched me in my gut.

That punch completely stopped my forward progress. I must have looked like a cartoon character—my body wrapping around his right fist, feet off the ground, then falling flat on my back. I lay there stunned and gasping for air.

I thought Scott might feel bad for me because I had had the wind knocked out of me. Instead, he jumped on top of me and started screaming in my face. "You want to be a SEAL? You want to do this? You better stay right behind me! You better stay three paces behind me! Three paces behind me!"

Then he got up and started down the path again.

*I have to keep up with him*, I told myself as I rolled over and worked my way back to my feet, thoroughly convinced mercy would not be any part of the rest of our day.

My stomach ached from the punch, and I think I was groaning a little as I resumed my pursuit of Scott.

I caught up to him and remembered his words: "three paces behind." I would not fall one step farther behind him—and definitely would not get one step closer.

When I settled in behind him, he picked up the tempo.

"Three paces!" he would yell back to me without slowing. "Three paces behind me!"

Walkers and joggers on the trail were looking at us with "What's going on with these guys?" expressions as we ran past. I'm sure my grunts and groans raised their curiosity levels. I had completely lost sight of Seth by then.

I struggled to stay with Scott. I had never run so hard in my life, and I decided on that path that I would literally let my heart explode before I quit running.

I know the distance now because when we started working out together regularly, Scott and I ran the same path often. We ran two more miles at our flat-out pace. Scott later told me we were running better than a six-minutes-per-mile pace, probably around 5:30 or 5:45.

Finally, Scott slowed our pace until we walked to a stop, then sat down to wait for Seth to catch up. We had a while to sit there and wait.

To this day, that three-hour workout remains physically the single most difficult one I've had in my life. My lungs were digging deep for oxygen. My stomach hurt to the point of almost doubling me over. My legs ached.

Scott stared at me. It seemed like a long stare.

"Bubba," he asked, "if we had gone another mile or two, could you have kept up with me?"

The honest answer probably would have been no. Instead I gasped out, "Yes."

"How far would you have gone with me?"

I caught a breath.

"I would have died before I quit," I answered.

Scott simply shook his head. I wondered what that meant. I soon learned.

Following a few moments of silence—other than heavy breathing—Scott asked, "When is the next time you're going to be ready to do this again?"

"Whenever," I said.

"How about tomorrow?"

I nodded yes, but I just about died inside thinking about going through everything we had just gone through again.

Scott then began delivering a matter-of-fact analysis of me.

"You're a strong runner, and if you really could have kept going another mile or two, that's good. But you're going to have to work on your strength. Don't get too muscle-bound, though. Eat some steak, some tuna, and some bacon. That will help."

He suggested I add about fifteen pounds, up to about 160. He said once I started SEAL training, I would be spending a lot of time in cold water, and a thicker body would provide me much-needed warmth. Besides, he added, I would probably lose those fifteen pounds during training.

I soaked up everything Scott was telling me. Before he

even finished talking I had decided to start a weight-lifting program.

As our conversation continued, Scott pulled back his all-business curtain ever so slightly, and I got my first glimpses of the Scott Helvenston I would come to know. He explained why he had punched me without specifically bringing up the punch.

He said that after he'd been on TV, it was common for people to ask to work out with him so they could try to beat him at something. They wanted to be able to brag about defeating the celebrity former SEAL.

That wasn't why I had wanted to outrun Scott. But now that I knew more about his experiences, the punch began to make sense. It still hurt, though.

Scott looked down at my feet. I had been running in skateboard shoes.

"You shouldn't be running in those," he told me. "Next time I'll bring a pair of shoes for you—some hand-me-downs."

I looked up when he said that. He'd said "next time"—which meant I had passed his test.

## BACK FOR MORE

We met up the next day in the same parking lot, and Scott greeted me with a gift—size nine-and-a-half running shoes, the first real running shoes I'd ever owned—and the great news that our second workout would be nothing like the first. I assumed that meant no punch to my stomach, but I remained alert just in case.

Before we started working out, Scott told me I couldn't afford to be cocky.

"Don't ever think that you could beat me at any of these things," he cautioned. "I'm going to help you, and I'm going to train you, but you can't beat me at anything we'll do."

Not being cocky was a constant lesson Scott wanted to teach me. He had figured me out during our first workout, and my attitude always seemed to be his greatest concern about my desire to become a SEAL.

Our workouts continued for seven months. Seth joined us for many of them, still saying he wanted to become a SEAL, but never seeming to actually take a step toward becoming one. Another man who entertained ideas of becoming a SEAL showed up sometimes too, but Scott had obviously taken me on as his special project.

Scott wanted to help me with anything I needed to master to make it through SEAL training. So in addition to the workouts, he challenged me with a variety of activities. We would take his kayaks out into the Pacific and paddle up to eight miles. He introduced me to rock climbing. He even put me and the other guys through basic land navigation exercises, setting up a course for us with designated points we would have to locate in a predetermined amount of time. Land navigation didn't come naturally to me, but Scott was always offering tips in a way that implied he believed I had what it took to become a SEAL.

From time to time, Scott took me to Camp Pendleton to run the obstacle course. Whenever someone else would accompany us, I would defeat him but not Scott. Of course, no one ever beat Scott on the obstacle course.

About two or three months into our daily workouts, after a midweek run in Santa Monica, Scott asked me a question. "So, when are you going to get the ball rolling on becoming a SEAL?"

"What?" I asked.

"When are you going to go see a recruiter?"

"Well," I said, "I think it's about time."

I visited a recruiter that weekend and signed up.

A large number of people were joining the Navy at that time—even my drinking buddy Jammel had recently joined because he wanted to try to do something different with his life—so I was placed into their delayed entry program. It would be seven months before I could officially enter the Navy. But that actually came as a relief because it meant I could keep working out with Scott.

## BEHIND THE SEAL

By that point I had stopped being "Bubba" and had become "Junior." Scott called most guys Bubba, I had noticed, but I was the only person I ever heard him call Junior. He said he was old enough to be my father and I had become almost like a son to him.

Scott, in turn, had become like a second father to me. We wound up spending many hours after our workouts talking not only about what it took to become a SEAL but also about life in general. And even when we weren't talking, I got to observe him as a person. He would greet total strangers on the street. He would hold open a door for someone he didn't know, even if the person was fifty feet away and he had to wait. That's the kind of considerate, others-centered man he was.

One of the things that impressed me about Scott was how big a family guy he was. Although he and his wife had divorced, his entire life seemed to center on his son and daughter. He would bring them along to our workouts sometimes, and I loved seeing the three of them interact. Some days he would load kayaks into the back of his truck and take the kids for a day at the beach with their dad. When his kids weren't around, Scott liked to talk about them and the fun things they had done together or that he had planned for them.

There wasn't much Scott and I didn't talk about. He told me anything I wanted to know about training—especially the rigorous six-month BUD/S (Basic Underwater Demolition/ SEAL) course designed to turn enlisted men and officers into SEALs. But there was one area where he seemed to withhold information. He always danced around the question of what SEAL life was like, giving me no more of an answer than the one time he told me he didn't have the best relationship with other SEALs.

He said his main focus while he was a SEAL had been staying in top physical condition. When some members of his team would go out drinking at bars, he wouldn't go. He said that had led to questions about whether he was one of the boys—the camaraderie card. But that was about as much as he would tell me. It was as though he didn't want to tell me about life as a SEAL because he knew experience would be my best teacher.

One conversation I'll never forget is when Scott told me he was considering returning to Iraq.

This was widely reported in media accounts after Scott's death, so I'm not revealing any secrets in saying that Scott had encountered financial difficulties. He had been offered a contract with Blackwater USA, the private security firm that supported our military by providing highly trained security guards in Iraq and also helped train the Iraqi army and police. The money would be good enough to help Scott provide for his family, and the opportunity to return to Iraq also appealed to his patriotism.

Scott explained the potential dangers and difficult conditions involved. Finally he summarized: "I can basically keep doing what I'm doing now, Junior. Or I can go with Blackwater and make the money I need to make in a couple of months. So what do you think?"

"Do it!" I immediately answered. I just knew that he would go over there, take care of a bunch of terrorists, and return to detail his experiences for me.

He gave me a look that said I needed to grow up. "Look, Junior," he told me, staring directly into my eyes, "Navy SEALs are not superhuman like everybody thinks."

That was our last face-to-face conversation. Scott accepted the contract and headed to Virginia for training.

While Scott trained in Virginia, I worked out on my

own—up to eight hours per day. The lifeguards who became accustomed to seeing me work out at the beach sometimes asked me what I was doing. "I'm going to become a Navy SEAL," I told them. "Uh-huh," they would respond in a "Sure you are" tone of voice.

Scott and I talked a couple of times per week on the phone so he could check on me and make sure I was keeping up with my workouts. "All right, Junior," he said in one conversation. "It's about time for me to go do this thing, and you're about to go away to boot camp. By the time I get back, you should be ready for your BUD/S class."

I didn't know what to say to that. Scott's words made the whole thing so real.

"I want you to know something," Scott added. "I know you're going to make it. I've never said that to anyone I've ever trained, but I know you're going to make it."

He closed with words I've never forgotten, and never will.

"You're the first guy I've ever known who's going to go to BUD/S that I'd be very proud to say is one of my guys. All the other guys, I never wanted the instructors to know they trained with me. But I'd be very proud for them to know you're mine."

I felt like I had just been knighted. I couldn't believe he'd said that—it was the highest compliment he could possibly give me. In a way, earning Scott's approval made me feel like I had already made it as a SEAL. It definitely made me that much more confident.

That was the last time Scott and I talked.

## HITTING HOME

A week and a half later, I woke up and turned on the television and VCR in my bedroom to begin my morning workout. In my mind, there was no better way to start the day than with a rigorous workout, and there was no better workout than Scott's SEAL-inspired video.

I was nineteen days from leaving for Navy boot camp, but I had been training for months with aims far beyond that. I was determined to become one of the elite, the best of the best—a SEAL. As far as I was concerned, Scott had been the ultimate Navy SEAL. The best of the best of the best. And he had become my friend.

As soon as I pushed the tape into the VCR, Scott's face would appear on the small TV screen in my bedroom, and we would begin yet another workout together. It wasn't the same as all the days we had raced across the sandy Southern California beaches or persevered through the rugged Camp Pendleton obstacle course or paddled kayaks along the Pacific coastline. But following Scott's directions through the television would have to suffice until he returned from serving out his contract in Iraq.

Perhaps I was moving slower than usual after crawling out of bed that morning. For whatever reason, the TV image came on before I inserted the videotape. And there was Scott's picture on the screen, staring right at me with that steely, military look that shielded the softer side of the Scott I had come to know—a playful, loving father who would do anything for his two kids and his country.

I wondered why he hadn't called me to say, "Junior, I'm going to be on TV today. Look for me."

Then, down at the bottom of Scott's picture, I noticed his birth date. Followed by a dash. Then another date.

March 31, 2004.

The evening before, while passing through the living room to the garage to grab the kayak Scott had given me for my solo workouts, I had heard from the television that four Americans had been ambushed and killed in Iraq. My mother had stopped me just long enough to ask, "What if that's Scott?"

"Not a chance. Don't even worry," I assured her, and continued to my workout.

Scott was still superhuman from my perspective, even though he had tried to convince me otherwise. Invincible. There was no way any Iraqi insurgents—no matter how many there were—could get to him.

I fell to one knee as news video replaced Scott's picture on the TV screen. My other knee dropped to the carpet. My arms draped straight down. It was as though my muscles had frozen and my eyes had locked in on the television. I don't know how long it was before I blinked, but my eyes filled with tears as the video rolled.

The footage was gruesome, unlike anything I had ever seen.

The Iraqis had ambushed the two vehicles containing Scott and the three other Americans. The video showed their bodies. I knew which one was Scott's by his forearms. Those forearms had motivated me during our workouts. *I want my forearms to look like that*, I would think when my arms were screaming, "No more!" Then I'd push myself to do even more pull-ups and push-ups than I thought I could.

Now Scott's sculpted forearms were limp. Lifeless. There was blood on his shirt. And his head . . . it still hurts to picture the damage from the gunshots.

Surrounding Scott was a mob of celebrating Iraqis, including kids who couldn't have been more than ten years old. They torched the two vehicles with the Americans' bodies still inside.

*Scott's on a supersecret mission*, I told myself. *He's just faking his death. Soon he'll call to say he's still alive and can't talk about it now, but I don't need to worry about him.*

It didn't work. My mind could no longer reject what my eyes were seeing. That was Scott, and what I was watching was real.

The Iraqis dragged the bodies out of the flaming vehicles and began beating them with rods. Then they tied ropes around the Americans' feet and dragged them behind vehicles through the streets of Fallujah. At the end of the video, the bodies—charred and mutilated—hung upside down from the Euphrates River bridge as the Iraqis gleefully chanted, "Fallujah is the graveyard of Americans!"

I heard someone coming down the hallway toward my room. My mom opened the door, crying.

"I'm so sorry," she said.

I looked up at her.

"Get out," I said. "Get out."

She turned and closed the door.

I spent the rest of the morning in my room, in shock. I wanted to be alone. I certainly didn't want to talk to anyone about what had happened.

Only a few hours later, though, I found myself in a conversation I didn't want to have. My parents, still stunned at Scott's death, cried as they tried to convince me to change my mind about becoming a SEAL. Aubrey and I weren't together at that point, but once she found out about my decision, she was really upset too.

Even though my parents had observed how I had kept my commitment to working out with Scott and had steadfastly worked out on my own after he had left for Iraq, their opposition to my joining the military never wavered. Seeing what had happened to Scott only intensified their fears of what could happen to me.

"Don't do this," my parents pleaded with me. "We can get you out. You don't have to do this."

The next day, the video of Scott and the others being burned, dragged through the streets, and hung upside down from the Euphrates River bridge was all over the Internet. My parents tried to get me to watch the video again.

"Look at this," they told me. "That's Scott. Please don't do this."

But I wasn't listening. Anger mixed with my sadness, and that anger was driving me.

I felt myself change as a human being. It felt almost as though Satan himself had entered me.

Where once I had asked myself, *When I become a SEAL, could I kill someone? Could I really do that?* now my thoughts were, *All I want to do is go kill. I want to kill everybody who hurt my friend. That is my goal in life.*

I had no fear; just pure rage. The two years of training to get to Iraq would be way too long. I was ready to go now. I wanted to know how I could find the names of the people involved in the ambush, how I could track them down. I wanted to go after them one by one until every one of them had suffered for his acts.

The two and a half weeks before boot camp are mostly a blur now. I try not to think about them because of the memories of how agonizing that time was. I cried every day. I didn't talk with anyone about what had happened because I couldn't do so without breaking down.

During my workouts—the ones that Scott had called me from Virginia to make sure I was doing—the images from the television drove me. I went drinking a few times, and when I drank, I descended into more of a rage. I was more determined than ever to make it through SEAL training so I could go to Iraq.

*We're going to have some revenge,* I thought. *We're going on a revenge mission, and we're going to get them.*

Whenever I hit a rough patch during boot camp or SEAL training, I knew what I would tell myself to persevere.

*I'm doing this for Scott.*

# CHAPTER 4

# CLEARING THE FINAL HURDLE

*Stay alert! Watch out for your great enemy, the devil. He prowls
around like a roaring lion, looking for someone to devour.*

1 PETER 5:8

★　★　★

**I HEARD BOTH** sets of footsteps coming down the hallway at
three in the morning because I was wide awake. My parents
were going to drive me to Aliso Viejo to report to the Navy
recruiter, and on my last night at home in my comfortable
bed, I hadn't slept a wink.

*Here we go*, I thought. *I'm really going away.*

Other than my sport-fishing trips and the two out-of-
state trips back in my skateboarding days, I hadn't been away
from home for anything. None of my siblings had left home
yet either. I was the first to leave, headed first to Illinois for
eight weeks of boot camp, followed by another eight weeks
of technical training in Virginia.

"Chad, it's time to go," Mom said as she and Dad opened my bedroom door.

"I know."

I wasn't all that excited about boot camp. I didn't care about basic training; I wanted SEAL training. Boot camp to me was nothing more than a step I had to take to achieve my goal. I might even have viewed boot camp as more of a speed bump than a step.

I finally started getting sleepy during the half-hour car ride. My parents wanted to talk, knowing this would be their last chance to speak to me in person for months. But I was thinking only of myself that morning, and I didn't want to talk.

"I'm tired," I told my parents, then laid my head back and closed my eyes as though I were trying to grab a short nap. I wasted our last moments together.

I kept thinking of my girlfriend, Aubrey. We had met and started dating about two years earlier, and even though we had an on-again, off-again relationship, I really liked her. My long trips on the fishing boats were part of the reason we had trouble staying together. My immaturity at the time certainly contributed as well. Every time we broke up, we eventually realized we couldn't really stay apart, and we'd get back together.

It was during one of our "breaks" that I had enlisted in the Navy. We'd gotten back together while I was in the delayed entry program, and now here I was leaving her. I had heard how difficult military duty can be on marriages, so it seemed to me that the risk of our relationship ending was even greater.

*I don't want to leave Aubrey.*

But then I would think of my fallen mentor.

*I've got to do this for Scott.*

I still hadn't fallen asleep when we arrived at my recruiter's office.

I say "my recruiter," but I hadn't really been recruited by anyone in the Navy. I'd recruited *myself* into the Navy.

It seems funny now, but when recruiters from the different military branches visited our high school, I'd had no interest in hearing their sales pitches. Now here I was walking into a Navy recruiter's office and saying good-bye to my parents.

I had seen many tears on Mom's cheeks since announcing my intention to become a SEAL. But that day, in that office, for the first time I saw a hurt look on my dad's face.

Suddenly I felt horrible. I had just blown off my parents during the car ride, and they were hugging me good-bye. Mom was crying, and Dad was telling me how much he was going to miss me. As I watched them walk away, I couldn't wait for my first chance to return home so I could apologize for everything I had put them through.

But I had been passed on to my recruiter. As I followed him inside, I recalled that the first time I'd entered into this office I had made a misstep.

The weekend after Scott asked when I was going to sign up, I had come to this very office, the one where my friend

Jammel had enlisted a week or so earlier. There was a US flag just inside the entrance. I didn't know that I was supposed to turn to the flag, salute, and ask permission to come aboard. I just walked in, right past the flag.

"Salute the flag!" the officer barked.

I saluted, but the wrong way. There was slack in my muscles, and my arm angle was awful. A toddler probably could have offered a better salute.

That led to a lesson on how to properly salute, with the officers giving me a hard time throughout their teaching session. Being a cocky kid, I got a bit ticked at being treated like that.

I looked at the officers chastising me, and they were chubby. I had been hanging out with an elite Navy SEAL who had put me through the workout wringer and given me a passing grade, and now I was being yelled at by out-of-shape guys who spent most of their time sitting at desks. I thought I deserved better than that—I told you I was cocky back then. In fact, I was about to tell them off when something inside me flashed up like a red light.

Instead of mouthing off, I just told the officers I was there to enlist.

Their tones immediately changed. They told me they thought I was someone who had already enlisted and should have known how to enter the office properly.

I wound up getting the same recruiter Jammel had signed up through, and he played all buddy-buddy with me.

"What do you want to do in the Navy?" he asked.

"I want to be a SEAL." I informed him that I had done the research, that I knew all about the contract that would promise me an opportunity to go through SEAL training after boot camp, and that I was ready to sign up.

The recruiter, though, seemed to want to build a rapport with me. He started telling me all the things I already knew, trying to sell me on something I had already decided to purchase. It was like entering a car dealership and saying you were ready to buy a particular car, then having the salesman go into his pitch and insist you take a test-drive.

The recruiter started telling me about SEALs he had worked with, how he had wanted to become a SEAL, yada yada yada. All I wanted to do was sign up and get out of that office and away from that recruiter. Instead, I was stuck sitting at his desk listening to his stories. Finally we made it through the chitchat and paperwork, and I was able to enlist.

## "PIER" PRESSURE

After my parents left me in Aliso Viejo, my recruiter drove me to a hotel in San Diego where a bunch of other recruits were gathering to leave for boot camp the next day. At the hotel I met up with one of my best friends since junior high, Brent.

When I decided to become a SEAL, I hadn't told any of my friends. But it just so happened that the day I visited the recruiter's office to sign up, Brent had enlisted with the Navy at a different recruiting office. Without knowing each other's intentions, we'd signed up on the same day and would be going to boot camp together.

When I found out that Brent had enlisted, I started trying to persuade him to become a SEAL with me. "You don't want to go be a nothing in the Navy, do you?" I asked him. "Go for the best. Become a SEAL."

Eventually, Brent decided he would give it a try. Not only would we enter boot camp together, but we would also be a part of the same class for SEAL training.

We didn't know if we would be able to spend much time together at boot camp, so we spent that night in the hotel hanging out, reminiscing about our good times together and speculating about what boot camp would be like. As we talked, Brent scribbled on a piece of paper. He handed me the sheet when he left for his room.

Brent had written the date—4/20/04—and "USN" for United States Navy. He'd added a few silly, short phrases from our past and some drawings of memorable events we'd shared. I had to laugh when I saw his drawing of the pier.

Huntington Beach has a really big pier—more than 1,800 feet long, about twenty-five or thirty feet above the water, with a restaurant at the end—that offers a dazzling view of the Pacific Ocean. Tourists and residents alike frequent the place, and lots of people go there to fish or watch surfing competitions.

Brent and I individually had a propensity for doing crazy things. Put the two of us together, and we were likely to do something really crazy. One day during my year in college,

I suggested to Brent that we jump off the pier. Pier jumping was a misdemeanor, but that hadn't stopped me before.

"How cold is the water?" he asked.

According to the surf report, it was fifty-three degrees, but I decided it was best not to tell him.

"After we jump off," I began telling him as someone who had made the jump dozens of times without getting caught, "all you've gotta do is swim in to shore. The cold water's going to shock you when you first hit it, but then you're going to catch your breath and you'll be okay. But when you're swimming in, whatever you do, do *not* grab onto the pylons. They've got barnacles all over them, and they're sharp. If you grab onto one, it's going to cut you up, and you won't feel it because of the cold. If you need help, just yell for me."

So we jumped in together, hollering "Banzai!" and "Cowabunga!" during our free fall.

I was pretty comfortable in the water because I surfed a lot and was used to the cold. Brent seemed to be doing fine too as we started swimming. I was cruising in well ahead of Brent when I turned my head to look back at him. I couldn't believe it. He was hugging a pylon!

"Don't do that!" I screamed at him, but it was too late.

Not only that, but Brent's grabbing the pylon had attracted the attention of a surfer, who hurried over to help him.

*Don't let him help you!* I was thinking. *You're drawing attention to us!*

The next thing I knew, a lifeguard was running toward the surf to rescue Brent.

I was close enough to the beach that I could stand in the water. "He's fine! He's fine!" I yelled to the lifeguard. "Don't worry about him."

Then I turned toward Brent. "Brent! Get over here!"

It was too late. Brent was already playing the role of victim in need of rescue.

The lifeguard brought Brent to shore, and Brent had blood all over him. His cuts weren't deep, but the water caused the blood to spread, making the wounds look much worse than they were.

The lifeguard started cleaning up the blood and applying bandages to Brent. By that point, a crowd of people had gathered on the pier and were pointing down to us. I could hear voices saying, "That's them," and "They're the ones who jumped."

"Brent," I said, leaning in close, "we've gotta run."

"No, man, I can't," he told me. "I can't. Go without me."

I had already committed to the SEAL creed: "Leave no man behind."

"I'm not leaving you," I told him. "Come on. Let's go."

"I can't, man," he said. "I just can't."

The lifeguard must have been getting suspicious because he said, "Both of you, stay right here." Other lifeguards were on the scene now, and they had kind of surrounded us with their vehicles.

I told myself that they had not collected any information from us yet and that nobody knew who we were, so we could still get away. But Brent wasn't budging. I think our fines were $110 each, and we were warned that if there were a next time, the fines would be much steeper.

## WORKING THE SYSTEM

It probably was a good thing for Brent and me that we were placed into separate divisions when we arrived for boot camp at Naval Station Great Lakes north of Chicago. Even then, we managed to get into trouble together. When we were in formation and came across each other's division, we would call out, "Hey, Brent," or "Hey, Chad." Or we would make faces at each other. That would cost us an extra round of jumping jacks or push-ups.

Getting in trouble during basic training didn't bother me. In fact, I often purposely got myself into trouble. My bad attitude about boot camp didn't diminish after I got there. To me, boot camp was just something I had to go through in order to get to SEAL training.

I'd hate to hear what some of the guys at boot camp thought of me, because I didn't make many friends there. Drew Lester is the only person with whom I developed what I would call a true friendship. Drew and I still talk on the phone from time to time, and he'll mention someone from boot camp he has talked to and ask if I remember him. "Nope," I'll say. "I don't even remember our drill instructor's name." Drew will bring up something that happened while we were there, and I'll have no memory of the event.

The truth was, I didn't make friends because I had no desire to. For the most part, I looked down on the other guys in our division. I considered myself different from them. Better, even, because I was the only one of the sixty-two guys in our division who was on a SEAL contract.

The way I looked at it, boot camp was the pinnacle for those guys, their "big thing." It was the make-or-break moment in their Navy careers. For me, it was something I had to endure to get to where I wanted to be. My mind-set was one of merely putting in my time and being along for the ride.

Besides, some of the things that we were told were so important seemed silly to me—such as ironing our underwear, then folding it just so. Or folding the small amount of excess space in our pillowcases the required way. We would shave twice a day not because we needed to, but because we were told to.

"If you pay attention to the details and fold your laundry the right way here," our drill instructor would say, "then we know that you can pay attention to detail when it comes to bigger things."

*Whatever*, I would think.

Now, if a SEAL had told me the exact same words, I would have been concerned about every detail. But my instructors weren't SEALs, and I didn't respect them the way I should have. I saw them as having settled for less.

The workouts at basic training were much easier than what I had been through with Scott and then on my own. Our instructors would assign us maybe thirty push-ups, thirty jumping jacks, and a mile-and-a-half run. Some of my workouts back home had included a swim of up to two miles, an eight- to twelve-mile run, and five hundred push-ups. I felt like boot camp was actually causing me to fall *out* of shape.

For that reason, I would do something like mess up my bunk before inspection or look an instructor in the eyes, which we weren't supposed to do. Such an act might earn me twenty extra push-ups. They were intended as punishment, but to me they felt more like a reward.

An instructor would light into me with, "You did five things wrong, and each of those is worth twenty push-ups."

I would think, *Sweet! I get to do one hundred push-ups!*

If I laughed a little, that would really upset the instructors, and they'd give me more "punishment." I did so much extra physical training as punishment that I picked up the nickname of "PT Nazi."

One day, though, about halfway through my eight weeks at boot camp, I didn't prepare my pillow to specifications. I didn't fold the wool blanket on my bunk the way it was supposed to be folded, and I pulled a corner of the sheet off the bed so that the plastic underneath was exposed. Then I stood next to my bunk as though I were prepared for inspection.

The drill instructor chuckled when he inspected my bunk. "You did this on purpose, didn't you?" he asked.

"Yes, petty officer," I replied.

The instructor ordered me down to the floor into a push-up position and walked away, leaving me there in that pose for half an hour. Later, he called me into his office and pulled out some paperwork.

He pointed to a blank spot for a signature on one of the pages and smirked.

"This is all I have to do," he informed me. "I can sign right here and totally cancel your SEAL contract. It says you're unfit to go into the SEALs."

"All right," I conceded. "I'll work with you."

He had me, and it bothered me to know that the drill instructor—someone who hadn't become a SEAL—had the power to take away the one big thing that I wanted to pursue. I realized the instructors had gained leverage, so for the rest of my time there, I begrudgingly played by their rules.

*I've gotta put up with it,* I told myself. *I've gotta put up with these guys.*

There were two times during boot camp when I was able to meet with a SEAL motivator. A motivator is typically an older SEAL who no longer works on teams and is nearing the end of his time in the service. He is someone who has been there and done that with the SEALs. His job is to take SEAL candidates from the various divisions and put them through a sampling of SEAL training.

The two times I got to work out for the motivator with the other candidates were the highlights of my time at boot camp. I wanted to work with the motivator more, but doing so required permission from the division petty officer. I had rubbed him the wrong way too, and he certainly wasn't interested in granting me any favors.

## HOME AT LAST

The end of boot camp appeared to be an emotional moment for everyone in the division but me. At the completion of training, our hats that read "Recruit" were replaced with hats emblazoned with "Navy" in gold letters. The instructors shook all our hands, and officially, we were no longer recruits. We were sailors.

They played a video accompanied by an emotional song, and I looked around to see most of the new sailors crying. I felt so different from everyone else. I knew I was on a different path.

Honestly, I can't say that boot camp had a profound influence on my Navy career. I didn't come out with respect for any of my instructors—primarily because I had gone into boot camp without respect for them. I only made one true friend, Drew. And the basic training was, as it says in the title, *basic*.

In addition to the proper way to make beds and fold and iron underwear, we learned how to march at a certain step and how to execute group maneuvers. We were placed in a gas chamber room into which CS gas (commonly known as "tear gas") was released, and we had to put our gas masks on quickly. That was one of the bigger moments for most of the guys, who would talk afterward about "getting gassed at boot camp."

We learned how to fight fires and dock boats, although it wasn't a real boat and it was a dry dock. Toward the end of our time there, we took part in team-building exercises, especially problem-solving situations such as repairing holes in leaking boats.

From my research and conversations with Scott, I knew the types of activities and exercises that I would be doing during SEAL training, and that knowledge made the basic training of boot camp boring for me. I couldn't wait to get started on what I had entered the Navy to do.

The best part of boot camp graduation was that my parents came, even though I didn't get to spend much more than an hour with them. We had what was called a "grab and go" graduation because afterward we had to immediately fly out to Norfolk, Virginia, for A-School, where new sailors receive their technical training.

In other words, I had another eight weeks of training to endure before I could get down to what I really wanted to do. Even though I had signed up to become a SEAL, I still had to select a specialty as a fallback in case I didn't make it. I knew that most would-be SEALs wind up not making it, but again, there was no chance in my mind that I would be one of those.

I put minimal thought into determining my specialty and selected OS, or operations specialist, because it sounded cool. No joke, my thought was that I would become "a specialist at operations." An operations specialist, I soon learned, works in the nerve center of a ship, operating radar, navigation, and communications equipment. When I discovered that was what I'd be learning, I thought, *You're kidding me.*

It was an eight-week training program, but when I arrived at A-School, the Navy was trying out a new computerized program that allowed trainees to learn their specialties at their own pace. I was motivated to learn as quickly as I could, primarily because I wanted to get out of A-School and into SEAL training. Thus, I would cram and memorize just enough to pass the test.

*When I'm done with A-School*, I thought, *I'll never deal with this again.*

I was through with the training within four weeks, although I'm glad I never had to put into practice what I (didn't) learn at A-School.

Even though I had finished early, I still had to wait in Norfolk to receive my orders. I wanted out of there so badly, and waiting on my orders was tough. I wanted to get home. Finally my orders did come through, and I was on my way home for the first time since leaving for boot camp four months earlier.

As our plane approached John Wayne Airport in Orange County, I looked through the window and saw the 405 Freeway and other landmarks I recognized.

*Yes!* I thought. *Finally!*

My parents and Aubrey met me at the airport, and it felt so good to embrace them. I hadn't seen Aubrey since my going-away party before I left for boot camp. I sure had missed her, and it was nice just to be in my home again.

I had a couple of weeks of leave time before reporting for SEAL training in San Diego.

"See, that wasn't so bad," I told my family. I knew I'd

be close to home during training and, except during Hell Week, we'd be able to make trips back during free time and on weekends.

But I wasn't really thinking that much about the weekends. I was looking forward to my SEAL training.

This would be my big moment.

# CHAPTER 5

# BRING ON BUD/S

*Don't you realize that in a race everyone runs,*
*but only one person gets the prize? So run to win!*

1 CORINTHIANS 9:24

★  ★  ★

"**LOOK AT THE** guy to your left. Look at the guy to your right. Look in front of you. Look behind you. Take a mental picture."

I looked around, my mind snapping pictures as the instructor at the front of the classroom paused. I caught Brent's eye from across the room, and he shook his head slightly.

"If you make it through BUD/S," the instructor resumed, "chances are, all those other guys you just looked at didn't make it."

That moment was a reality check for me. We had been told repeatedly that the large majority of us would not make it to the end, and some of the 173 in our class had already decided to drop out during Indoc. When I surveyed the classroom, I remembered hearing each man declare that he would die before he quit SEAL training.

Many of those guys looked tough and, as far as I could tell, no different from me. I wondered whether I was really going to be tougher than the guy to my left. And the one to my right. And the ones behind me and in front of me. I knew I wouldn't quit, but those around me seemed like the type who wouldn't quit either.

*Wow*, I thought, *where are those quitters going to come from?*

It turned out that they would come from all over the room. About a year later, at the end of our training, only thirteen of the original 173 would have persevered all the way through to our SEAL class's graduation.

BUD/S (Basic Underwater Demolition/SEAL) is the six-month SEAL training course that is equal parts training and elimination. It is considered the most difficult military training program in the world. Each BUD/S class takes a couple hundred aspiring SEALs and breaks almost all of them down to the point where they just cannot go any further—ensuring that those who do get through will be physically and mentally fit for the most extreme challenges.

## SNEAK PREVIEW

I was fortunate to receive a sneak preview of BUD/S. My report date was ahead of most of our class, and we early arrivers were shipped out to San Clemente Island. This Navy-owned island northwest of San Diego is where the final phase of BUD/S training takes place and also where SEALs go through advanced land training.

Though the activities on San Clemente Island are usually shielded from the public eye, the place wasn't entirely unfamiliar to me. I'd seen parts of the island on a Discovery Channel special that documented the journey of a SEAL training class. And our sport-fishing boats had often anchored off the island, where we glimpsed tantalizing signs of activity.

"What's going on?" I remember asking.

"The Navy SEALs are out there—that's them training," the veteran fishermen would tell me. Most of the SEALs' activities took place at night, though, so we couldn't really see much.

One of my captains told about a time when he heard noises in the middle of a pitch-black night. He looked down and was startled to see SEALs in the water around his boat. "Shut up," the SEALs told him before disappearing back into the water.

There is a lot of mystery surrounding San Clemente Island.

When the other trainees-in-waiting and I arrived at San Clemente, it was a ghost town. There was no BUD/S class training there, just the five of us plus an instructor. The instructor was very relaxed—we didn't know yet how rare a sight that was—because we didn't have any business to tend to there.

For almost a week, we lived a life of leisure on the island.

We swam in the ocean, we went spearfishing, and we climbed cliffs and spotted sharks. I was thinking I could get used to that kind of Navy lifestyle. But our vacation ended when the current BUD/S class showed up for its final phase of training.

I remember watching them arrive in their brown T-shirts. At the beginning of BUD/S, all trainees wear white T-shirts. At the completion of Hell Week, the few remaining in the class are rewarded with brown shirts to signify they've survived the toughest week of training.

After that, we trainees stayed busy with chores—picking up trash and brass (discharged gun shells), delivering coffee to instructors on the shooting range, and performing range watches to make sure no one ventured down roads where they were in danger from live fire. We had minimal interaction with the brown shirts themselves, but we did get to observe them. And believe me we did, because they were where we all intended to be in a matter of months: on the homestretch to becoming SEALs.

We spent five weeks on the island before reporting to the Naval Special Warfare Training Center in Coronado, California, where the majority of our BUD/S training would take place. I had already had a foretaste of the NSWTC, too, because it's located on the Naval Amphibious Base Coronado, where Scott Helvenston had taken me to run the obstacle course.

Before beginning BUD/S, we went through a sort of preBUD/S called Indoc—short for Indoctrination. In Indoc we learned the evolutions, or exercises, we would be put through during BUD/S. We also learned the rules and procedures of BUD/S and the basics of SEAL swimming techniques and tasks, like underwater knot tying. We started off walking the obstacle course to learn the different skills required to complete it, then advanced to running the course. We became acquainted with the small rubber boats that would come to feel like part of our bodies.

Indoc also afforded us an introduction to life as a SEAL and the SEAL creed: "Leave no man behind." Adhering to that creed requires that SEALs always be able to account for one another and that a SEAL leader be able to keep track of exactly how many men are with him. The harsh consequences for failing to do so start immediately, with extra physical training and a verbal dressing-down from instructors as punishment.

The physical training of Indoc served as an equalizer among the trainees. Those who were not in the best physical condition found that PT raised their conditioning level. For those who arrived in tip-top shape, like me, it provided less of a workout than we were accustomed to and brought our conditioning down closer to the level of the first group.

Regardless of what condition we were in when we reported or how fit we thought we were as Indoc wound down, there was no way to be fully ready for the actual start of BUD/S.

Nerves were obvious on the first morning of BUD/S as we classed up, or divided into assigned groups, and tackled our first assignment: painting our helmets.

We had to paint our helmets green—the color symbol of

First Phase of BUD/S. Then we added white stickers showing our class number, 254, and our last names. The paint job and sticker placement had to be absolutely perfect. Any blemish resulted in a hit. Three hits equaled a fail. Fails went on your record and resulted in extra physical training.

The required attention to detail was no different from what had been preached to us at boot camp. But because this was SEAL training and where I wanted to be, I paid attention to the details.

My helmet passed inspection. So far, so good.

## WELCOME TO BUD/S

It was five o'clock in the morning, still dark, with a chilly, damp wind blowing off the Pacific. We stood outside our barracks, anticipating that something big was about to happen but clueless as to what that might be.

*Vroom! Vroom! Vroom!*

Many of our instructors rode motorcycles, and we could hear their engines roar ahead of their arrival. One voice piped up from within our group: "The demons have arrived, and we're about to go through hell."

"BUD/S Class 254, get over here! On the grinder! Now!" an instructor barked through a bullhorn.

We immediately dashed to the grinder, a large concrete-asphalt area where calisthenics took place. That's the nice way of putting it. To be more descriptive, the grinder is where we went to get "ground." Many an exercise beat-down took place there.

On the grinder, the instructors sprayed us down with water hoses before ordering us to "Hit the surf!" We sprinted over the sand berm that separated our training center from the beach and began our first surf torture.

I believe surf tortures are now referred to as "water immersion." I guess the word *torture* didn't look good to the public. But it's an accurate description of what it was like in that cold ocean water.

Here's how it worked. At the beach, the instructors had all of us line up with our backs to the water and gave us the order, "Link arms!" We linked arms with the guys on either side of us. Then we had to do an about-face and link arms again. The next command was, "Forward march!" Arms linked in one long chain, we marched into the water as waves crashed into us.

We continued marching until the water was chest high and the instructors ordered, "About-face. Take seats!" We brought our legs up into a sitting position. The waves gradually carried us back to shore until our bodies were scraping the sand. The waves continued to slap us in the face, and with our arms still locked, there was nothing we could do to block the slaps.

Sand got into our eyes, up our noses, into our mouths, and inside our ears. It worked its way through our fatigues and into our armpits, our groins—any and every place it could affix itself. This is known as "getting wet and sandy." When we came out of the ocean, instructors made us roll along the beach until we wore a thick coat of sand from head to boots. If we didn't get enough sand on us, instructors would be in our faces, yelling at us to get down and pick up more sand before linking arms and heading back into the water for another surf torture.

The sand was irritating, but what I struggled with most was the cold. It was late January. I had wanted to go through a wintertime BUD/S because its Hell Week is considered the most difficult one and offers the most bragging rights to those who persevere through it. But at that time of year, the water temperature ranges from mid- to low-fifties, the air temperature from the mid-fifties to mid-sixties. And for me that made surf tortures the most difficult of all the evolutions we were put through.

I had followed Scott's eating tips, but I just couldn't manage to put on the pounds, so I still weighed about 145. I excelled at exercises such as running, swimming, pull-ups, and push-ups because I had less weight to carry than most of the guys in my class. But because I had little body fat, I felt the extreme of the cold sooner than others. I was one of the first to start shivering during surf tortures, and I took longer to warm up afterward. I quickly learned to link arms with one of the larger guys, hoping I could feel a bit of his body warmth. You'd be amazed how much just that little extra bit of warmth helped.

With the cold air and water, the annoying sand, the seemingly endless surf tortures, and the constant yelling, the instructors tried to weed out the weaker trainees within the first hour.

"We just want three quitters," the instructors told us. "Three quitters, and we'll take you out of the water."

What we didn't know, and I wouldn't learn until well after I'd finished my training, was that the instructors had charts that, based on the water and air temperatures, guided them on the maximum amount of time they could safely leave us in the water. I'm sure they were taking us right to the limit, but we were unaware that such a limit existed. As far as we knew, the instructors really would keep us in the surf until they found their three quitters.

That was one of the psychological games the instructors played with us, and the games worked. Two or three guys gave up right off the bat. I could only surmise that the anxiety—all the talk they had heard about how demanding BUD/S would be—got to them. They probably experienced those first few hours and couldn't imagine multiplying that short amount of time into two or three more weeks just to get to Hell Week.

To be honest, seeing those first guys quit was a relief to me. Not only did it get me out of the surf that first day, but it also made me more self-confident to know I had already begun to outlast some of those tough-looking guys.

Those who quit during BUD/S—quitting is officially called Dropped on Request, or DOR for short—don't just walk away. They are required to return to the grinder, where a brass bell hangs outside the First Phase office. Each recruit must give three solid tugs of a short rope to ring the bell loud and clear, then place his helmet on the grinder and head off for a lesser Navy assignment than he had planned for when he signed up to become a SEAL. Everyone can hear the bell ringing throughout the training compound, and let me tell you, whenever that bell sounds, everybody stops what he's doing to listen for the full three-gong knell—the one that identifies a quitter.

As the days of training accumulated, so did the number of helmets on the grinder.

It has been said that ringing the bell is the most humiliating experience a man can ever go through. It is so humiliating that the Navy actually removed the bell for a few years. It was brought back, though, and I believe it is there to stay.

It is common to see a guy cry as he rings the bell because he feels like such a failure or to see someone ring the bell so reluctantly that an instructor gets in his face and orders him to ring it "like a man." Some trainees delay quitting to put off the humiliation, although their helmets eventually join the growing line. One person ringing the bell often opens the floodgates for others who want out but are waiting for someone else to drop out first. I've heard of guys who were discharged from the Navy because they were deemed mentally unfit to serve after going through the trauma of ringing the bell. There are even stories of those who became suicidal after dropping out of SEAL training.

Ringing that bell was never an option for me. Not once during my training did I think about voluntarily dropping out. But I did consider the possibility that something beyond my control—a severe injury, for example—might prevent me from completing training. If that had happened, I had decided I'd go AWOL—just leave the base and head straight to nearby Mexico. If I couldn't be a SEAL, I wouldn't stay in the Navy. That's how much the SEALs meant to me.

Giving trainees every opportunity to ring that bell is as important a part of the instructors' jobs as preparing future SEALs for combat. With the dangerous missions SEALs are called upon to carry out, there is no room for anyone who might quit when a situation goes bad. When facing enemy gunfire in a war zone, a SEAL needs to know that the fellow SEAL assigned to cover his back in the heat of battle has stared into every logical reason to ring that bell and defiantly said no.

The grinder and surf tortures were a rude awakening. They did their job of making me wonder what months of that same kind of training would be like.

But I didn't even want to look at that brass bell.

## THE POWER OF FEAR

After our first surf torture, we ran to chow. We always ran to chow. It was a mile to the chow hall and a mile back. With three meals per day, that was six miles of running only for meals—and those miles didn't count toward our conditioning runs.

Timed four- and eight-mile conditioning runs were standard. There were days we ran close to a full marathon in addition to all the other evolutions. We didn't make those runs in T-shirts, shorts, and running shoes, either. We did everything in standard uniform—jungle camouflage tops and bottoms, white T-shirts, thick socks called "dive socks," and Bates military boots. (I would have preferred running in my skateboard shoes again.) We also always wore caps, which were attached to our camo tops by a red lanyard so we wouldn't lose them.

Running on the loose sand of a beach is difficult in itself. It's really difficult in boots. But the ocean water that soaked our uniforms added more weight, and the sand chafed our skin. All that discomfort would be our way of life for the rest of training.

There was only one part of our early BUD/S training that I really liked: surf passages. It involved our IBSes, or "Inflatable Boats Small." An IBS is a rubber boat about thirteen feet long and weighing 150 pounds when dry and empty. Ours were rarely dry and empty. The ocean water kept them wet, and the instructors kept them from being empty by using a wooden oar to shovel sand into the boats for extra weight.

We usually had teams of six men for each boat, and those boats basically accompanied us everywhere. The fun part, though, was taking them out through the surf zone, which is the impact area where the waves break on the water as they come in. We had to maneuver our boats through the incoming waves and past the surf zone, flip the boat over so we would be familiar with how to pull off that maneuver when we had a boat filled with water, then return to the shore and do it all again. And again. And again. For a surfer like me, riding vertically up the waves on our way out was a blast.

We first did those evolutions during the daytime, but once all the crews had become accustomed to negotiating the waves, we were set for our first surf passage at night. Our section of the West Coast gets pretty big waves during the winter, so I was excited.

"Oh man, we're going to have a really good time," I told the others. "We'll get to see some serious waves. This will be fun."

Some didn't buy what I was selling, especially those who hadn't grown up around an ocean. Before we set out for our night surf passage, I saw fear in the eyes of guys who had proved themselves to be physically and mentally tough to that point. They were getting psyched out, and some were crying and saying, "I can't do this. I can't do it." The surf tortures, the push-ups, the pull-ups, the instructors yelling—they had lasted through all of those. But the thought of going out into complete darkness to confront waves we wouldn't see until they hit our boats—it got to them. A handful quit before the evolution began.

For me, though, the nighttime surf passage was as much fun as I had anticipated. The waves sounded bigger than normal that night—one instructor said he saw one wave reach about twenty feet—and they were doing a real good job of tossing us out of our boats. We would get knocked underwater and have to hold our breath for fifteen or twenty seconds as waves rolled over us until we had washed back to the shore.

Although I was surprised at some of the guys who let the waves psych them out, I could understand the fear of those who hadn't grown up around an ocean. Watching those who quit before even confronting the first wave was an attention-grabbing demonstration of how powerful fear of the unknown could be. I just had an advantage because surf wasn't an unknown to me.

Drownproofing was another exercise we learned early on. At least this training took place in the calm comfort of a swimming pool, but it was still a challenge. One thing we had to learn during drownproofing was how to bob in water. The instructors would basically hog-tie us—bind our ankles together and our hands behind our back. Then we would jump into about ten feet of water. Our arms were useless, and we could only use our feet and legs to push off the bottom of the pool. We had to drop slowly to the pool's floor, then push ourselves back to the surface and grab a quick breath. We would repeat the same down-and-up process for ten to fifteen minutes.

In order to descend all the way to the floor, we had to exhale all of our air out so that we were no longer buoyant. Otherwise, with air-filled lungs, we would have remained near the surface. I would desperately want to take a breath as I slowly sank to the bottom, but I couldn't take one until I had reached the floor and sprung back up to break the surface. My mind had to prevent my body from doing what it naturally wanted to do.

At this point we were also tested on skills we had begun

practicing during Indoctrination. Underwater knot tying and the fifty-meter underwater swim were now make-or-break—three failures and we were out! For the fifty-meter underwater swims we would jump into the water, do a flip, swim twenty-five meters underwater to the far wall, and return to the other end before breaking the surface for air.

The underwater swims were a piece of cake for me. I could have done them all day, another advantage of my Southern California upbringing. But some of the others became overwhelmed and called it quits—or their bodies called it quits for them. The instructors called it "red-lining"—losing consciousness underwater before making it to the finish. The instructors would pull their limp bodies out of the water, get them breathing and back to consciousness again, only to inform them, "Hey, dummy, you failed. That's one strike against you. And you know it's three strikes and you're out!"

The most dangerous evolution in BUD/S was the rock portage. It started like a surf passage, with each boat crew taking its IBS out past the surf zone. But then, instead of turning back for shore, we continued toward a rock jetty near the famous Hotel del Coronado. Needless to say, the hotel guests were enjoying slightly more luxurious conditions than we were.

At an instructor's signal, the crew paddled toward the rock pile—some rocks were the size of small cars—and had to negotiate the surf to land the boat on the rocks and pull it ashore. After three successful landings, the crew had to maneuver the IBS back over the rocks and launch it right into the face of the surf. We repeated that exercise until the instructors decided we knew what we were doing. From there, we moved on to nighttime rock portages.

Teamwork and timing were critical in that evolution, and injuries such as deep bruises, sprained ankles, and cracked bones were not uncommon. The instructors warned us repeatedly never to allow ourselves to be caught between our boat and the rocks. One misstep and a big wave could bring us face-to-face with one of those big boulders, and the boulders always won. Medical personnel were always on hand and at full watch during rock portages.

Like most of our training, the rock portages had a specific purpose. They were examples of the kinds of missions Navy SEALs are expected to execute during combat. When there is a large stretch of sandy shore, an enemy expects us to land there. Coming in at night on a rocky portion of the shoreline gives us the best shot at gaining the element of surprise.

## SUFFER IN SILENCE

An incident at the rope-climbing station taught us early not to expect mercy during training.

After a few boat-crew races through the surf zone, the instructors decided to take the class back across the sand berm to the climbing station for a crew-against-crew rope-climb race. The race was about to kick off when we heard one of the BUD/S mottos: "It pays to be a winner."

Instructors rewarded winning crews during competitions

by allowing them to sit out the next surf torture or evolution. (Second-place finishers were referred to as "first losers," so it only paid to win.) Such a rare physical break was well worth putting in a winning effort.

Our hands were so cold and numb from being in the water that it was difficult to even make a fist, let alone grip a rope that became wetter and sandier with each person who climbed it. I was fast at the rope climb, so I was the last to go for our crew—the anchorman. The other crew's anchorman was named Stewart. His team was ahead of ours as he began the climb, but not by far. I started gaining on Stewart on the way up, and he saw me coming.

Stewart's crewmates cheered him on because they wanted to enjoy the benefits of being winners, and he probably felt the pressure to hold the lead. We had made it to the top and back down to about twenty feet from the ground when I saw one of his fingers give on the rope. Then the entire hand lost its grip, and Stewart went zipping down the rope, screaming all the way. When he struck the ground, I heard the snap of a bone breaking. Stewart hollered in pain as he squirmed on the ground, grabbing the injured leg.

I hung on to my rope momentarily, not knowing what to think or do, then slowly—and carefully—resumed my descent. Before I reached the bottom, Stewart had been surrounded by instructors. They ordered everyone to turn their backs and face away from Stewart, and then they began yelling at him.

Stewart was still screaming in pain, and the instructors

were yelling above his cries, "Shut up!" and "Stop being a sissy!"

*His leg is obviously broken,* I thought, *and all they can do is yell at him?*

"Suffer in silence!" they commanded Stewart, repeating yet another SEAL mantra.

They never once asked Stewart if he was okay or showed any concern.

After medical personnel took Stewart away, the instructors told us to shut up and said it was time to get busy again—as though Stewart's injury was just an annoying glitch in their schedule.

"Stewart is out of this," they said. "Get over it, guys. He's done. He should have held on to the rope."

I understand now that the instructors' attitude was part of our training. A SEAL wounded or injured in combat could endanger others around him if he screamed in pain, potentially revealing the SEALs' location. That's part of the rationale behind suffering in silence.

Our instructors had all experienced combat. I assume they all had seen fellow team members severely or even mortally wounded, and some probably had buddies die right next to them. A broken leg suffered on a training course must have seemed relatively minor to them, because a broken leg would heal. What really mattered was preparing us for life-and-death situations.

Stewart's injury definitely clued us in to the level of expectations the instructors had for us. They weren't going to listen to any whining or crying. They just expected us to put up with whatever happened to us.

I wondered if I was on my way to becoming just like those instructors. In that moment I couldn't imagine being with someone who had just suffered what seemed like a gruesome injury and not showing some concern for his well-being. But perhaps someday I would react as the instructors had.

*I'll probably become mentally tough like them*, I thought.

Then my mind turned to my fear of an injury like Stewart's that would prevent me from being able to complete training.

*That's exactly what I don't want happening to me.*

What caused Stewart to fall was in his control, but then again it wasn't. That incident reminded me that I was one slipped finger away from seeing my dream come crashing down.

Or maybe just a simple trip to Medical would do it.

At the time, I was battling through what I thought were shin splints. My lower legs were so sensitive that it hurt just to touch them with my fingers. Even my toes touching the floor when I got out of bed in the mornings sent pain shooting through my legs.

I say I *thought* I had shin splints because I never went to Medical for an official examination. I didn't want to risk a diagnosis that might take me out of the program. So like most of my fellow trainees, I would answer, "Hoo-yah, sir, I'm fine," when an instructor thought I looked hurt and asked if I was injured. ("Hoo-yah" is a SEAL phrase used to express enthusiasm or even as a yes or no answer.)

We weren't allowed to take any supplements or over-the-counter pain relievers that did not come from Medical. Getting caught with prohibited medicines or supplements would have gotten us kicked out of training. Yet it also wasn't worth the risk of getting kicked out by going to Medical for a few pain-killers. So like many others, I took the "suffer in silence" principle seriously and never complained about being hurt.

I did, however, eat lots of dried cherries. I had heard that eating a bunch of dried cherries has the same effect as taking ibuprofen. After I told my parents about my shin splints, they kept me well stocked in cherries. I don't know if the cherries helped with the pain or not, but I was willing to try anything to relieve the pain—anything short of going to Medical. It crossed my mind that I might continue to train until I fractured one or both of my legs. Yet I was willing to take that risk over asking for medical help.

I wasn't going to be leaving training on my own, and I sure wasn't going to give a doctor a reason to remove me, either.

## SURPRISE BELL-RINGER

More than twenty members of our class DORed in the first few days of BUD/S. After that, it seemed like we lost ten to fifteen more each day, so that by the end of the first week, just over one hundred members of our class remained.

A pattern emerged. One person would say he was considering quitting, and others of us would encourage him to stay. "Don't do it," we would urge him. And that person might hang on for another evolution, maybe even two. A few would stick it out until the next day. But I noticed that once the idea of quitting had been planted, that was it. Not one person who admitted he was thinking about quitting ended up staying, no matter how hard we tried to convince him. It wouldn't be long until he walked away, making that humiliating trek across the beach and toward the berm.

Even with their backs to us as they walked, we could tell some of the quitters were sobbing as we yelled, "Come back! Don't go!" But they would disappear over the berm, and we would soon hear the bell ring three times. *Bing! Bing! Bing!* The next time we returned to the training center, their helmets had been added to the line that stretched its way farther and farther along the ground.

Seeing one helmet in that row rocked my world: Brent's.

The instructors figured out early in BUD/S that it was good to keep Brent and me separated. We were always looking for some kind of prank to pull. When a guy would drift off during a break or in a classroom, we would pour water on his pants and tell him he had wet himself while he was snoozing. We were always joking around with other trainees, picking on them or hassling them for any reason we could find—or make up, if we needed to.

Brent and I were the first in our class to have a nickname pinned on us by the instructors: Prom Boys. Somehow the story got to instructors that Aubrey and I had invited Brent to tag along with us to her school's homecoming event. Even though it wasn't a prom, the instructors ran with it and began calling us the Prom Boys.

Before they started splitting us up, Brent and I were swim buddies. SEALs always have a swim buddy, and the concept of a SEAL never being alone is so important that I don't think it's possible to get into more trouble for anything during BUD/S than for getting separated from a swim buddy.

Instructors liked to single out Brent and me from among the swim buddy groups, and we were usually the first to be called out. "Where are my Prom Boys?" an instructor would ask. The instructors never missed an opportunity to pounce on a mistake we made so they could try to embarrass us in front of the class. They also attempted to make our tight friendship work against us.

"We're going to make both of you guys quit," an instructor would snarl into our faces.

We would simply smile, knowing that they couldn't make us both quit.

After the instructors split us up, they played mind games with us. "Hey, your brother just quit," an instructor would tell one of us.

We never believed them.

"Hey, man!" I'd tell Brent when we met back up as a class. "They tried to tell me that you quit!"

"Yeah," Brent would say, "they told me you quit too! I didn't believe it."

I think the instructors actually liked us. They certainly got enough free entertainment from calling us Prom Boys. But their job was to see who could consider every reason to quit and then not do so.

Brent did well at the start of First Phase. He was great at running, push-ups, and pull-ups, and he was good enough at swimming. That's one reason I liked being his swim buddy; we worked well together. We were probably having about as good of a time together as could be had while spending an entire day running, exercising, getting beat up by ocean waves, having sand get stuck in places nobody wants it stuck, and being yelled at by instructors who were trying to make us walk out on our dream.

Near the end of our first week, we were introduced to an evolution called wet-suit appreciation. That was one of our toughest days, partly because it was one of the coldest. Our class was split into halves on different parts of the beach, and Brent and I were in different groups.

The instructors had placed buoys about a quarter mile out into the ocean—not far, really. "Go swim around the buoy," they told us, and we did. When we got back to shore, they said, "Go do it again," and we did. That cycle kept going for what seemed like forever.

We never had any idea how many more times we would have to make the swim in that cold water, but we assumed there would always be one more swim. Finally, the instructors ordered us out of the water. "Let's run four miles," they told us. When we finished that run, we were met with, "Do another five miles."

After that, we were handed wet suits—but not winter wet suits. These were spring suits, which covered our upper bodies but only went down to our thighs. They were also hand-me-downs, and wet suits do have a shelf life. My suit bore eight stenciled names that had been crossed out.

In those suits that had seen better days, and wearing fins called "duck feet," we had to swim out past the buoy and back with our swim buddies. It was practice for going through the surf zone.

We were supposed to stay within three feet of our swim buddy, and I was paired with a guy who wasn't a fast swimmer. I was getting slowed down by my partner, and the cold was getting to me. I figured that the quicker we finished our swim, the sooner we would be on dry land. We kept swimming the circuit over and over and over. I would grab my slower partner and actually start pulling him through the water so I could get an extra few minutes on the beach before returning to the cold ocean.

Then the wet-suit appreciation portion of the evolution began. The instructors told us to remove our wet suits and make the swim again.

Next, it was "Take off your T-shirts and do the swim." Eventually, wearing only our underwear, we made our final trip around the buoy.

I was even colder than usual from having circled the buoy so many times when the instructors sounded a siren to signal us to immediately come in. On the beach, the instructors told the boat-crew leaders to take charge of their men. "Get a head count of your guys and put your clothes on." My hands and fingers were so numb I could barely tie the laces on my boots.

When everyone mustered—or gathered back together to get accountability and find out who remained and who had left—word began circulating that Brent was gone.

*No, no, no*, I immediately thought. *The instructors are just messing with us again. They're hiding him from me so I'll think he quit.*

"Brent quit," a class member told me.

I didn't believe him.

The bell began ringing over the berm.

*Bing! Bing! Bing!* A short pause. *Bing! Bing! Bing!* Another pause. *Bing! Bing! Bing!* The bell kept ringing. Wet-suit appreciation had created a line of those who had had enough.

"Okay, seriously, where is Brent?" I asked the others.

"He quit, Chad," came the answer.

I was stunned. It had seemed like destiny that we would become SEALs together. We had gone through junior high and high school together. We had somehow enlisted in the Navy on the same day without telling each other our intentions, then wound up in the same boot camp and BUD/S classes. We had been beside each other every step of the way, and only a few hours earlier, Brent had told me that the instructors could never make him quit.

Brent and I didn't make contact with each other for probably three weeks. I think he actually avoided me for a time because I started calling his cell phone at the end of each day and could never reach him.

When we finally talked, he described how ashamed he felt about quitting. During wet-suit appreciation, he said, he just didn't think he could take it anymore. He became overwhelmed, went over the berm, rang the brass bell three times, placed his helmet next to the others, and returned to the barracks for a warm shower.

As soon as the warm water of that shower had melted away the cold, Brent started crying tears of regret. After the shower, while still in his barracks, he saw our class without him for the first time. Our torture was over, and we were preparing to run to the chow hall. Brent watched us on our way, realizing that things weren't so bad for us anymore, that if he'd just hung in there a little bit longer he'd still be with us, headed indoors for a warm meal.

Instead, he returned to the ocean side of the berm, lay on the beach, and wept.

Brent's leaving was the first big mental blow I suffered during BUD/S. He was like a brother to me, and I could feel his pain. I knew he would struggle with regret for a long time.

As those of us who remained after the wet-suit appreciation evolution ran to chow, I prayed aloud, "O God, please help me, God. Please help me."

If Brent quit, I knew I would need the help. I would need more strength than I possessed to make it through Hell Week.

# CHAPTER 6

# HELL WEEK BEGINS

*When you go through deep waters, I will be with you. When you go through rivers of difficulty, you will not drown. When you walk through the fire of oppression, you will not be burned up; the flames will not consume you. For I am the LORD, your God, the Holy One of Israel, your Savior.*

ISAIAH 43:2-3

★　★　★

**THE ONLY SOUNDS** were crashing waves, the ocean breeze pecking at our tent, and the softened voice of someone occasionally asking when Hell Week would begin, followed by a "Shut up! I'm trying to sleep."

*Ba-ba-ba-ba-ba-ba-ba-ba-ba-ba-ba-ba-ba-ba!*

Out of nowhere, the startling racket of machine guns surrounded us. Instructors burst into our tent screaming, "Go get into the surf! Hit the surf! Everyone into the surf!"

Splashes of flares across the sky burst through the late-night darkness as we sprinted into the surf for a quick dip before being commanded to run for the grinder.

Oh, the grinder. We knew it was coming even before

we made it all the way into the ice-cold waves of the Pacific Ocean.

There was all-out commotion at the grinder. Grenade simulators exploded all around while instructors fired blanks from fully automatic machine guns. Even though the bullets weren't real, the noise they made going off right next to our ears sounded like the real deal. The warmth of the shells hitting our skin as they were discharged from the instructors' weapons offered a stark contrast to the cold water we'd just left.

The brass links that had connected the rounds skittered under our feet as we raced around the grinder, trying to stay with our boat crews as instructors attempted to disorient us and separate us by grabbing trainees and trying to hide them from their crews. "Where's your boat crew? Are you missing someone?" the instructors kept shouting.

Then everyone was ordered to do push-ups or pull-ups or organize as a boat crew and pile into our boats. Then it was out of the boats while instructors tried again to disrupt each boat crew's accountability. The only thing we knew for sure was that whatever anyone anticipated would happen next, would not happen next.

And during all this pandemonium, on the decks of the two-story complex surrounding the grinder, intrigued onlookers calmly watched as we scrambled to stay together.

There is a fascination with Hell Week that generates the curiosity of friends and family members of people at the military base. They want to see for themselves whether the "breakout" of a Hell Week is as jarring as they have heard it described. It didn't go unnoticed by us that as we entered the first stage of the most difficult week of military training in the world, we were also serving as a form of entertainment for the people who had gathered. And they, unlike us, had known when it was going to start.

No other military, including the other branches of the US military, has a Hell Week as intense as the one that Navy SEAL trainees encounter. Portions of our Hell Week have been copied and adapted, but no one has developed a training course on the same level.

Hell Week is five and a half brutal days of sleep deprivation, nonstop shivering from hours spent in the ocean water, and running around with a boat on top of your head until you develop bald spots and then scabs on skin rubbed raw until it opens and bleeds.

Hell Week is designed to bring trainees as close to combat experience as possible without placing them in a war zone. The goal is to generate more physical and mental stress than any trainee will ever face in combat—to prepare the future SEALs for anything and everything they might eventually encounter.

While the opening weeks of BUD/S are focused on increasing physical stamina and improving skills while weeding out the mentally and physically weak, Hell Week goes a step further: it eliminates anyone with an ounce of quit in him. The belief, supported by years of combat experience, is that those who can make it through Hell Week without quitting will not quit in combat when conditions become difficult, when their buddies need their backs covered.

The first dose of Hell Week includes the element of surprise. Trainees know as they begin First Phase of BUD/S that Hell Week typically starts sometime in the third or fourth week, but that's as specific as the information gets. For our class, it was the third week.

We had spent part of Sunday in the classroom, continuing the same training topics of the first two weeks. And by that point, the classroom reeked. Whenever the instructors gathered us in that room, we were almost overwhelmed by our own musty, grimy smell. But we didn't mind the odor as much as might be expected because the heat from our soaking-wet bodies helped warm up the room. I wouldn't be surprised if our collective body heat raised the room temperature ten degrees.

Following that Sunday of typical BUD/S evolutions and activities, we were sent to a large tent on the beach. Sensing that our Hell Week was possibly about to begin, most of us tried to grab a quick nap. Who knew when our next chance to sleep would be?

Except I couldn't sleep. I was so anxious about the approach of Hell Week that I closed my eyes but couldn't close my mind enough to fall asleep. There was a sense of excitement inside the tent, probably because the others who couldn't sleep were thinking the same thing I was thinking.

*In a little less than a week, Hell Week will be behind me.*

## THE STAR BURNS OUT

One of the traditions during BUD/S is that as a class nears Hell Week, trainees write motivational words underneath the bills of their caps.

I wrote a series of words and phrases.

"Family."

"Scott Helvenston."

"Aubrey."

"Friends."

And in confident anticipation: "Hey . . . I made it!"

I even added, "It's okay. Jesus is on my shoulders." It wasn't that I spent that much time thinking about Jesus. But I had grown up in a Christian home and had gone (reluctantly) to a Christian school, so the lingo came naturally to me—especially now, when I was facing something really big. I thought I needed to cover all my bases.

That just about filled the underside of my bill. But knowing what was ahead of me—that I would really need the strength I had prayed for after Brent DORed—I decided I should have something else related to God on my hat.

Philippians 4:13 came to mind. I remembered hearing family and friends quote that verse throughout my life, and it was one of the few verses that carried any kind of meaning to me. Of course, I didn't have it memorized. All I knew was "I can do all things through Christ" (NKJV). So I found a Bible, looked up the verse, and wrote the entire thing out on the top of my bill. I couldn't see it there, but knowing that

I had in some fashion acknowledged God made me feel even more confident than I already was.

Interestingly enough, that Scripture ended up getting me into trouble, not out of it. One of the instructors noticed the writing on the top of the bill (rather than just the bottom) and lit into me on the grinder at the start of Hell Week.

"What is this on top of your hat?" he yelled into my face, creatively sprinkling his words with profanity.

I hadn't thought he would be able to read the writing with the darkness and all the commotion. I started to explain what was there. That was a mistake.

The instructor grabbed the red lanyard that connected my cap to the front of my uniform top. The lanyard wrapped around my throat, and the instructor kept pulling on it, yelling and cursing at me.

At first I was surprised. Then the pressure from the lanyard began to hurt to the point that I thought it was going to cut into my skin. The instructor turned the lanyard loose, and I dropped. But the yelling and cursing didn't stop.

"What is this writing? What is this writing?"

Without looking him in the face—I wasn't about to give him another reason to reach for my lanyard—I told him, "It's about Jesus. And about Scott Helvenston."

Scott's name seemed to be the one in that pairing that he most respected, because when I mentioned Scott, he left me alone.

We spent probably an hour on the grinder before the instructors ran out of blanks to shoot and grenade simulators to set off. Either I was becoming accustomed to the yelling or the instructors were getting tired, because the volume of the orders seemed to have lowered.

Then we were ordered back across the berm to the beach. I knew what was coming. *Here we go*, I thought.

Our class was divided into two, and each half was sent to a different part of the beach. Then, as I'd guessed, we were commanded to link arms and march out into the ocean for a surf torture. But it soon became clear that these surf tortures would be different from those of the previous two weeks.

Up to that point, we'd had breaks from the harsh cold. Surf tortures would be followed by activities on land so that when we did go back into the surf, we had some warmth built up. Plus, we would usually stop after three or four surf tortures in a row.

I can't recall how many surf tortures we did at one time during Hell Week, but I know it was much more than three or four. They seemed endless. And the cold never stopped. Even when we were out of the ocean, the instructors would hose us down with cold water, so we were already cold when we started up a new round of surf tortures. It just so happened that the temperature dropped during our Hell Week, so the water hovered around fifty degrees.

Less than fifteen minutes into the first of our Hell Week surf tortures, I started shivering. From then until after Hell Week ended, I don't remember a time when I wasn't shivering.

From the very first day of BUD/S, I had hated surf tortures. Now, as determined as I was to make it through Hell

Week, I could barely endure them. Having sand in my eyes and not being able to do anything about it drove me crazy. The cold seeped deeper and deeper into my bones. And the instructors kept yelling nonstop, urging us to go ahead and do what seemed inevitable—quit.

Hell Week's first round of surf torture is known for its ability to collect more than its share of bell ringers. At first, no one quit. But as the surf torture began to drag on longer than it had the first two weeks, the quitting began.

The instructors had been nice enough to make it easier to DOR. The bell had been mounted on the tailgate bed of a pickup and conveniently brought to the beach—the only time the bell ever left the grinder back at the compound. Those who wanted out didn't even have to make the walk over the berm and back to the grinder.

"Why don't you just quit? Why don't you guys just go quit?" the instructors kept urging us. "You can go take a warm shower right now. This is just the very beginning of Hell Week. Do you really think that you can do another five and a half days of this? You guys aren't going to get any sleep. Just make it easy on yourself right now."

The instructors never relented.

"This is your way out! We have a hot meal ready for you! We've got some warm hot chocolate for you! Why don't you just quit?"

Before long, the bell began to ring. We would watch someone ring the bell, then another would walk away, then another. But we had no way of knowing exactly who had quit until the two groups of us were brought back together.

That's when I learned that Ben had rung the bell.

Ben was the star of our class. When our class had first assembled at the beginning of BUD/S and we had surveyed each other to identify who we thought would make it and who wouldn't, Ben had been pegged as a can't-miss.

This was Ben's second time in a BUD/S class. A few years earlier, he had made it to the second day of Hell Week before he DORed. He had spent the time since on a ship. But when offered another opportunity to become a SEAL, he'd jumped at it.

Knowing what he was about to encounter, Ben came prepared, reporting to BUD/S in great physical shape. As competitive as I was, I soon learned that the best I could hope for was second place in every physical contest—runs, swims, pull-ups, push-ups, you name it. Ben was so far ahead of the rest of us that he truly was in his own league within our class.

Because Ben had been through what we all were just beginning, he quickly became our go-to guy. He readily answered our questions and guided us through the first two weeks of BUD/S. So we were stunned to learn he had quit. He hadn't even made it as far into Hell Week as he did on his first attempt.

I never talked with Ben again, so I do not know what happened. Perhaps because he'd endured those two days of Hell Week before, he knew what was coming and decided he didn't want to go through it. Whatever the reason, knowing our number one guy had quit made a significant psychological impact on our entire class.

Ben's departure really opened the floodgates. There always seemed to be safety in numbers when it came to dropping out. One would leave, then it seemed there were three or four who'd been waiting for someone else to make the first move. But when Ben left, at least twenty guys followed him. Maybe they'd planned to quit anyway and felt better that they had at least outlasted the star of the class.

For some, just making it into Hell Week seemed to be an achievement. I remember talking to one guy during the first week of BUD/S who had been in a previous BUD/S class and almost made it to Hell Week before quitting. He told me that this time he hoped to at least make it to Hell Week. "At least that would be respectable, to quit then," he explained.

But I didn't get it. To me, his mentality seemed to be the complete opposite of what anyone in a BUD/S class should have. Just making it to Hell Week before quitting didn't seem respectable to me. It certainly wasn't an option I let myself consider. In fact, I was noticing a strange thing about myself. When guys quit—except for Brent—it didn't bother me. Instead, I felt stronger, as if I'd consumed whatever amount of power they had left behind. I gained confidence when others left. *He quit?* I would ask myself. *At that?*

In the time since I finished SEAL training, I have taken part in many conversations with other SEALs and former SEALs about Hell Week. Each has talked about one recognizable point where he thought he couldn't make it. It almost seems therapeutic to them to gather and talk about the one moment that almost did them in. But I never had one of those moments. Most SEALs don't believe me when I tell them that, but it's the truth. I never came close to quitting. I would not allow that thought even to enter my mind.

The way I looked at it, there was no way out of Hell Week. Not even that stupid bell was a way out. To me, it was almost like I'd been placed in a concentration camp. Prisoners of war who are thrown into concentration camps have no way out. They have no other options than to be there, to take whatever punishment is handed out to them, and to survive.

That is the attitude I adopted. I never allowed myself to think that I was volunteering for Hell Week. A volunteer can leave at any time he wants, but in my mind I couldn't do that. There was no door. Hell Week became something I had to do and had to live through.

I would never try to pretend that Hell Week was remotely easy. It remains the most difficult experience—physically and mentally—of my life. Nothing else has come close. I can't report what methods others from our class used to make it through Hell Week, but I do know from watching those who left that the path to quitting is permanently paved when someone allows quitting to become an option.

## ONE NIGHT DOWN

After that intense first surf torture, the instructors sent us back to the other side of the berm, where a moat had been dug out to protect the training-center buildings from any waves that topped the berm. Water would accumulate in the moat because it had nowhere to drain, and vegetation had started to grow in the stagnant water.

"Into the moat," the instructors ordered us.

This water was noticeably colder than the ocean water, and it smelled much worse than our classroom. I've never heard of another SEAL class spending time in the moat like we did, so I hope that our experience at least put an end to that practice.

The instructors made us low-crawl through the moat, dropping completely flat to the ground and crawling around and around the moat, over and over and over. It was so cold in the moat that the wet sand from the beach actually felt warm to us, at least serving as a layer of insulation for our bodies. When our shoelaces came undone and an instructor yelled at us to retie them, our hands were so numb that it sometimes took two or three guys working together to tie someone's laces. Guys were so cold that they would jackhammer, or shake almost violently.

When I was in the moat, I couldn't wait to get out and do some type of physical activity—regardless of what that activity was—to raise my body temperature even the slightest bit. I actually preferred surf torture over the moat. That's how horrible it was.

After our first session in the moat, we crossed back to the ocean side of the berm to head for a landmark that locals know as the elephant cages—a giant, circular antenna setup that had once been used to provide communication for submarines. To get there, we took what was known as the elephant run, a six-mile trip down the beach. We left behind the base and the lights of civilization for a remote place where it would be just us and our instructors.

We made the run with our boats. We carried our boats just about every place we went during Hell Week, either on top of our heads or at our sides, using handles.

I was motivated during the elephant run, and I knew our instructors wanted to see us encouraging our teammates. So I ran my mouth as much as I ran my feet.

"Here we go, guys!"

"You got it!"

"Let's keep going!"

"We're doing good!"

That upset the boat leaders, typically officers who were expected to be doing all the leading. I found out later that instructors would pull boat leaders aside and ask, "Why is Williams leading your boat crew? Why aren't you?"

Boat leaders actually came up to me quietly, away from the instructors, and told me to tone it down because I was making them look bad. I would stay silent for a while, but I couldn't stay that way for long. The encouragement was as much for myself as it was for others.

The leaders would get onto me again, and I wasn't going to take it quietly. "Well, you need to step it up then," I'd shoot back at them.

At the end of our six-mile run, we had to enter the water

with our boats and paddle a couple of miles to a jetty for a rock portage and a landing of our boats at the rocks.

The sun was getting close to showing itself by now. It hadn't come up yet, but the sky was changing colors ahead of its arrival. I remember thinking, *Wow, we've already made it through the night, and the sun is coming up. We've already survived one night.*

We had made it to Monday morning.

## MILE BY LONGEST MILE

After bringing our boats ashore, it was time for our first meal. So we sat down to eat—in the fifty-degree ocean.

Most of our meals the first two days were MREs—Meals Ready to Eat. These are rations packaged to be eaten during combat or in other field conditions where a "real" meal cannot be prepared. We received two MREs each at our meals during Hell Week to replace the large number of calories we were burning.

MREs will never make it onto the menu of In-N-Out Burger, and some believe eating them qualifies as torture itself. But none of us thought that during Hell Week. Not when we had surf tortures to compare them with. And our first full day included plenty of those. After all, what would a day of Hell Week be without more surf tortures than we could count?

The instructors resumed their psychological games. After we completed a surf torture, they ordered us to take one boot off, then get back into the water for another torture. Then we took off another boot and got back into the water. Then we removed a T-shirt, and so on until we were doing surf tortures naked. As long as we still had a piece of clothing on, we knew the surf torture wasn't about to end. But once all our clothing was gone, it became another guessing game as to when the instructors would end the evolution.

That drawn-out process caused a few more guys to quit.

The rest of the day was spent running around either with boats on our heads or carrying logs—telephone poles that were about the same length as an IBS (Inflatable Boat Small) and weighed at least as much.

We kept running laps with boats and then poles and then boats and then poles until the sun went down. The instructors allowed us to stop long enough to take note of the disappearing light and, as a group, wave good-bye to the sun.

Guys continued to DOR throughout the evening and night.

By that point, I had learned to narrow my perspective to the task at hand. It was too challenging to think, *I've gotta make it through this day*. It was better to think, *I've gotta make it through this one evolution*. Then I would do the same with the next evolution. I wouldn't think any further ahead than that. And I never thought about the remainder of Hell Week. If I had done that—and I suspect this is what happened to those who were dropping out—I easily would have become overwhelmed by what lay ahead.

As the week progressed, I began thinking in even shorter terms. While running along the beach, *I've gotta make it through this evolution* eventually became, *I've just gotta make it to that seaweed on the ground.* To think *I have x number of days or x number of miles to go* would have guaranteed that the task ahead would overpower me.

One reason I sliced the challenges ahead into small pieces that I could actually see ahead of me, such as with the seaweed, was that part of the instructors' psychological strategy was never to tell us when an evolution would end.

A good example of this strategy was what we called "the longest mile." A regular mile wouldn't even be considered a warm-up for how much we ran during our longest mile. Just before our longest mile began, the instructors made another attempt to get inside our heads. The sun was going down, and a shift change brought on a fresh set of instructors. They commanded us to line up along the ocean's edge facing the setting sun. Shivering from the cold, we were ordered once more to wave good-bye to the sun.

"Buh-bye, sun," one instructor said as we waved. "We will feel no warmth from you. It is going to be a very, very long and cold night without you. We will miss you!"

Then the instructor ordered each of us to say, "Buh-bye, buh-bye, sun. We will miss you."

That scene was oddly humorous, with us looking like a bunch of preschool kids waving farewell to the sun as it excused itself for the night. Then it was time for the "mile" that would wind up sending another large group to the bell.

We didn't know where or how far we would run, but we were told to start running back toward the base, which was six miles away. We left our boats behind and ran to the base, where we picked up logs and carried them the six miles back to our boats. Then we dropped the logs, picked up the boats, and carried them back to the base. And we kept doing that until the instructors finally told us our "mile" was over.

We did miss the sun. Even though we were cold and shivering during the day, the sun did warm us a little, and its light gave us a psychological lift. But when the sun went down each day, guys would mentally break.

Brief periods of inactivity hurt us too. When we stopped our evolutions to eat at night and our muscles calmed down from the lack of activity, that was when the cold really started getting to us.

The instructors would follow us around during Hell Week in several extended-cab trucks, including the one with the infamous brass bell that proclaimed the demise of so many trainees. The instructors brought the bell to taunt us wherever we went during Hell Week. To make matters worse, on one occasion they started offering warm ravioli to anyone who quit.

"If you want to quit, now's a really good time," the instructors kept saying. "We have the trucks here, and they have the heat on. It's nice and warm inside, and we'll get you guys inside that cab, take you back, and let you take a hot shower. Then you can climb into your warm bed and get some sleep."

Once the first person rang the bell and could be seen enjoying the ravioli inside a warm truck, it was another floodgate moment. The bell kept ringing at the hands of guys who were walking out on their life's dream for just a little bit of comfort in the cab of a truck.

So many people quit that night that they filled up the warm cabs. Some guys who had been promised a cozy spot in the heated truck in exchange for quitting had to settle for the back bed of a truck. But still, they were on their way out of the cold.

About this point I noticed a change in the attitude of those of us who hadn't quit. Where previously we had shouted encouragement to try to prevent those who wanted to give up from ringing the bell, we seemed to have stopped caring.

My attitude became one of, *Do whatever you've gotta do. Just go ahead and give up. I'm not even going to try to stop you.*

# CHAPTER 7

# WE DID IT!

*Don't be afraid, for I am with you. Don't be discouraged,*
*for I am your God. I will strengthen you and help you.*
*I will hold you up with my victorious right hand.*

ISAIAH 41:10

★ ★ ★

FROM THE VERY beginning of training, our boats had been part of every evolution. Although their official name was Inflatable Boat Small or IBS, they were often referred to as itty-bitty ships. And during Hell Week, we spent so much time carrying those itty-bitty ships around on our heads that they became like a home to us, much like a shell is for a turtle.

I mentioned earlier that we carried the boats so frequently that our heads developed bald spots, then scabs that would rip open the next time we took off on a run with our boats. We even ran our boats to and from chow and hauled them with us on obstacle-course runs. Since a boat weighed

150 pounds completely dry and empty—even more with the wooden paddles and the water and sand the instructors added—the load wore on our necks and legs, too.

Boat crews were sorted by height so that guys more or less equal in height were on a crew together. As the numbers in our class steadily dropped, we were constantly forming a new height line to divide into new crews of four or six guys. Each boat had a Roman numeral on the front, and each crew went by its boat's number—except for the boat operated by the "Smurf Crew." The shortest crew received the boat with the blue Smurf painted on the front.

When our class was full, I was about fifteenth or twentieth from the short end of the line. By the second night of Hell Week, because of the dropouts, I landed on the Smurf Crew. The Smurf Crew took a lot of ribbing—mostly good-natured, but not completely—and each Smurf Crew member took on a collective sense of pride, especially anytime the "little guys" outperformed the other crews.

Boat runs had a way of quickly revealing who the weaker guys were within the crews. When the load became too much for someone on the crew, he would duck his head a little—called "ducking boat"—to take some of the load off his head, neck, and legs. When an instructor saw that happen, he zeroed in on the ducker, getting directly in his face and yelling, "You're a loser! You're not supposed to be here! Why don't you quit now and make it easier on yourself?"

As the evolutions during Hell Week slowly passed, the

changes in our attitudes were especially evident in the way we treated boat duckers.

Early in Hell Week, when an instructor was reaming out someone on our boat, we would encourage our fellow crew member to hang in there and not quit. We would try to protect him as much as possible, positioning the boat so that an instructor couldn't see him ducking. Or when someone slipped out from under the boat to run a few steps beside it for a momentary break, we wouldn't say anything to him.

But gradually, as we began to realize how much extra weight a ducker was causing us to carry and how much we were being slowed, our level of concern for the ducker's needs disappeared. One person trying to get away with running alongside the boat would infuriate us. "Get back under the boat!" we would tell him. "Help us!"

The instructors were masters at poking at our growing impatience. Where previously the instructors were the ones trying to pressure the duckers into quitting, they instead began putting the pressure on the nonduckers. They aimed to create tension between us and the duckers that would cause us to force the duckers to head for the bell.

The instructors would turn from a ducker and tell us, as if we didn't know, "So-and-so is ducking boat on you. *He* is the one slowing you down."

It was one thing to have an instructor riding someone, but it was another when every other member of his crew started turning the screws on him. I compare it to when a splinter gets under your skin. When the skin reaches the point of being irritated, it builds up enough pressure to squeeze the splinter out.

The ducker was in a position where he really wasn't participating, but he didn't want to quit, either. So the members of a crew would run harder to try to get rid of him, all the while yelling, "Just get out! Get out of the boat!" I saw guys who would fall to the ground and get run over by their crew before they finally decided they'd had enough and quit.

The first time someone like that dropped out, the smaller boat crew actually became faster without him. That demonstrated to the rest of the crew just what kind of deadweight they had been carrying, and the tolerance level for future duckers diminished from there.

There was one instance in which we had two guys drop out of our boat during a run, leaving us with four. We had been in last place with a full crew, but minus those two guys we wound up winning all of our boat-crew races that night.

Watching the number of boats decrease gave a sense of just how many guys were dropping out. What once had been a line of fifteen boats was down to four by Wednesday. Barely more than twenty guys remained.

Those who make it into Wednesday of Hell Week most likely are going to make it through the end of the week. Those are the ones who have proved they really will die before they quit.

Looking back, I can see that Wednesday was a turning point. On that day the instructors seemed to take a slightly different approach with us. They had pushed us physically and mentally for three consecutive days. And although we had demonstrated that our bodies could accomplish more than our minds thought they could, advancing far past our self-set limits, the body still does have natural limits that cannot be exceeded.

We were told going into Hell Week, "The instructors will not kill you." And those of us who were still around—even though we probably didn't fully realize it at the time—had trusted the instructors with our lives. I don't underestimate the responsibility that SEAL training instructors carry. They could literally run a trainee to death.

On Wednesday, I realize now, the emphasis shifted from weeding out the weak to binding together those that remained. The emphasis was more on team building. But I couldn't see that at the time. It just seemed like more of the same.

Late Wednesday afternoon was also the first time since Hell Week began on Sunday night that we were given an opportunity to sleep. As welcome as sleep might sound, my first nap actually created my absolute most difficult moment of Hell Week.

Two hours of sleep time were allotted, although the boat crew that won the competition right before that naptime was the only crew that would have a full two-hour window for sleep. Hey, it pays to be a winner!

Our Smurf Crew was the last to the tent, so we had the least amount of time to sleep—a little more than an hour. When I woke up, I noticed the first swelling in my body. The sleep had signaled to my body that it had a chance to heal the muscle soreness from the three days of evolutions. When we were rattled awake with shouts of "Hit the surf!" I think every one of my muscles had drastically stiffened. The instructors were yelling for us to get up, and my mind was responding, but my body wasn't having any of it.

Instructors: "Let's go! Let's go! Hit the surf!"

My body: "Are you kidding me?"

Feeling how much my body ached as I rolled over to get off my cot and leave the tent, my mind realized that Hell Week wasn't over.

*Oh, no. We're still in this.*

My body was still shivering, and my spirits were down as I ran out of the tent.

"Come on, Williams, let's do this," the man next to me said.

It was Tommy.

I mentioned earlier that Ben was the one that I—and most others—had designated early on as our class's most likely to succeed. Shockingly, he had DORed early during Hell Week.

Tommy, on the other hand, was the one many of us had determined would be one of the first quitters, if not the first. He'd showed up a little overweight and looked like he was out of shape. He didn't appear to be athletic, and he was an admitted video-game junkie.

*He won't be here long*, I'd thought.

Yet there Tommy was on Wednesday of Hell Week, more than two days after Ben had left, and he was encouraging me!

Tommy's words and determination motivated me. My mind-set immediately shifted from *Here we go again,* to *All right! Let's do this!*

Tommy and I sprinted across the beach with the rest of the class and into the water.

## UNPLANNED NOSE JOB

From when I woke up after that nap through the end of Thursday, I don't recall much of what happened. I know we continued with many of the same evolutions we had been doing, but specific events and times of day don't stand out too well when I review Hell Week.

Even with the nap, the effects of sleep deprivation had kicked in. Plus, one of the ways our instructors would mess with our minds was to tell us the incorrect day of the week. I didn't need instructors trying to confuse me that way because my mind was confused enough on its own from the lack of sleep.

The second half of Wednesday and most of Thursday are fuzzy when I look back, but I do remember taking another short nap on Thursday. And I definitely remember what happened Thursday after that nap. The slight crook in my nose today serves as a reminder.

We were doing more boat-crew races and going out past a surf zone packed with good-sized waves. And I happened to be in position three at the time.

There are different crew positions in an IBS. The two guys at the front of the boat are in what is called position one.

The two guys in the middle are in position two, and the two guys in the back occupy position three.

As we would race to get into the water, the command "Ones in" was the signal for the front-row guys to jump into the boat and start paddling. When we got a little farther into the water, the middle-row guys would jump in on "Twos in." Then the same would happen for the back row.

I was in position three during one race when, right after we had all made it aboard, we saw a really large wave approaching. The timing on the wave was all wrong because we were just getting out to the bigger surf.

Our itty-bitty ship started going vertical. We were obviously not going to make it through that wave. But even in a situation like that, a crew has to commit to *try* to make it through.

One of the position two guys in the middle row didn't commit. Instead, he bailed out of the boat. That put the guy in position one on my side of the boat directly above me as we rode up the wave. He was hanging on to the boat, and I was at the very bottom.

I saw the position one let go. I had my oar in my hand, so I put it up in front of me to try to stop him as he fell toward me. He was larger than me, though, and all his weight coming down collapsed my extended arms. My paddle smacked across my nose with the added force from number one's weight.

Despite the noise from the wave and our yelling, I heard my nose crack.

The wave separated our crew members from the boat, and the boat made it back to shore ahead of us. When we were away from our boat like that, we would hold on to our paddles and ride the surf in.

When we reached the shore that time, we all ran to our boat as we were supposed to. I had blood from my nose flowing everywhere by that point, and the instructors saw it and came out to meet me in their trucks.

"What's going on?" one asked. "What just happened, you idiot?"

As I've said, no mercy.

"I can't breathe out of my nose," I answered.

The instructor looked at my nose from different angles. "Oh, yeah," he said. "That's broken."

I tried to look at my nose in one of the side mirrors of his truck, but he wouldn't let me.

"What, are you worried?" he asked. "Worried you're not looking like a pretty boy anymore?"

I wasn't concerned about my looks; I was curious and wanted to see which direction (or directions) my nose was facing.

The instructor grabbed my nose and moved it around. I heard crunching and cracking, followed by more crunching and cracking.

I began to be able to breathe through my nose again.

"You good?" the instructor asked.

"Hoo-yah!" I replied.

The instructor taped up my nose to make sure I could

breathe, and his overenthusiastic tape job earned me the nickname Hannibal Lecter for the rest of Hell Week. I thought it was funny, and so did the instructors. For the rest of Hell Week, the instructors would get my attention by saying something like, "Hannibal, get over here!" That was better than Prom Boys, for sure.

The nose wasn't a big deal. Sure, it hurt. But every part of my body was hurting by then. Even when I broke my nose, I never feared it could prevent me from finishing the week.

## SNACK ATTACKS

Thursday night was the start of the evolution called "Around the World."

Coronado Island sits across San Diego Bay from the city of San Diego. And although it's called an island, technically it's a long, thin peninsula connected to the mainland by a narrow strip of land at the far south end of the bay. Naval Air Station North Island occupies the north end of this peninsula. To its south lies the beautiful small city of Coronado with its luxurious resort, Hotel del Coronado. And south of the city is Naval Amphibious Base Coronado, which includes the Naval Special Warfare Training Center, where much of the SEAL training takes place.

Around the World is basically a long, long boat race. It starts on the ocean side of NAB Coronado, continues north along the western edge of Coronado Island, rounds the north point where the naval air station is, then continues down the bay side of the island and back to our training location.

The race begins at night and continues well into the next morning.

Because of sleep deprivation, I had been having hallucinations, especially at night, and even more so when we were in the ocean. During Around the World, I experienced the strongest hallucinations I have ever had.

I began to see the Teenage Mutant Ninja Turtles in the water. I used to watch those cartoon characters when I was a kid, and now I was sure they'd followed me to Coronado Island.

I would think I'd see one stick his head out of the water and smile at me. I would take my oar and slap the water where I saw Leonardo, Raphael, Donatello, or Michelangelo, but his head would duck beneath the water before I could hit him. I would row a little more before the next smiling Ninja Turtle would pop up out of the water, and I'd swing at and miss him, too.

Then I started seeing ninjas onshore, and things really got crazy.

It is a final-night tradition during Hell Week for the brown shirts of the previous SEAL class to sneak sweets and snacks to members of the current Hell Week class. Instructors are aware of the tradition, so it has become a sort of cat-and-mouse game between the brown shirts and the instructors.

The previous class decided to make their special delivery during Around the World. Our Smurf Boat was in the lead when the brown shirts, dressed in all black, appeared, running along the shore and past the lighted sections of a building. But in my confused state, I thought the black-clad figures were actual ninjas and that the building was the Japanese dojo where they trained.

I alerted my boat crew: "Look! Look! The ninjas are pouring out of the dojo!"

The rest of the Smurfs looked at me like I was losing my mind. (I was.) But I kept insisting that those were ninjas and that was their dojo. For some reason—perhaps their own sleep deprivation—the guys in the boat slowly started to at least partially believe my claim.

"We've gotta fight together," I told the crew, convinced our boat was about to be captured by the ninjas.

There was a low dock that ran out into the water, and the brown shirts ran out ahead of us and onto the dock. "Here they come! Here they come!" I hollered as we neared the dock. They were going to reach the end of the dock right as we reached it, and by that point we were standing in our boat, ready to swing our paddles at the invading ninjas.

But as we approached the dock, a black bag landed in our boat. At first, no one said anything. We just looked at the bag, confused.

"Hey, we're trying to help you!" one of the brown shirts shouted to us.

Then it finally hit us. Those were members of the previous class, and the black bag was our forbidden food.

We opened the bag, and the first things we pulled out were boxes of white powdered-sugar doughnuts.

It pays to be a winner, but we no longer cared about

winning Around the World. There wasn't an oar in the water as we ripped into those white-coated doughnuts.

Boat crews started passing us. Some asked, "What are you guys doing?" We didn't answer. We were too busy eating.

The brown shirts tossed goodie-filled bags to all the boats, but the other crews ate while they paddled. We dropped all the way from first place to last, but we were happy because we were loading up on doughnuts, cold pizza, Snickers bars, and Gatorade. Aware we were bringing up the rear, we had to start moving again, so we ate and paddled at the same time.

We knew we would soon be coming up on one of the instructors' checkpoints, and we also knew we were not supposed to have any of the food and drinks in our boats. We racked our fuzzy brains for a way to hide our treasure.

It was probably around two or three o'clock in the morning, so the bay was quiet except for our boats and our voices. We were approaching the lights of the docks and could see the instructors only fifty feet or so away.

"Hide the food," one of the Smurfs said just loudly enough for those of us in the boat to hear. Someone tossed the bag into the water, hoping it would stay afloat and we could reconnect with it after we passed inspection at the checkpoint. That bag was all we cared about right then.

At the checkpoint, we had to stand next to our boat at attention, eyes straight ahead. An instructor walked around the boat, kicking it to make sure it was still properly inflated and checking the insides for all the equipment we were supposed to have—and anything we weren't supposed to have—while hassling us for dropping to last place.

When we landed, I wondered if the instructor suspected we had been eating. After all, sneaking food was a final-night tradition, so he had to be expecting something. Then I stole a peek around me during the inspection. I saw some of the others looking around too, and it was obvious we were seeing the same thing.

Every one of us had white powder from the doughnuts on our faces.

We tried to subtly signal to each other about the evidence. The instructor—Instructor Stone—walked up to me, looked me over closely, and asked, "You got any contraband on the boat there, Williams?"

"Hoo-yah, Instructor Stone!" I answered.

By that point of Hell Week, if you've made it that far, you have become so stubborn and so hardheaded that you no longer fall for the intimidation act. There is *nothing* an instructor can do to get to you at that point, and they know there is nothing they can do that would make you quit.

So I flat-out denied it. "I don't know anything about any contraband on the boat, Instructor Stone!"

He wiped a finger across my face, put it directly in front of my eyes with the white powder evident, and asked, "What is this, Williams?"

"That must be dried-up salt water on my face, Instructor Stone!"

He knew I was lying, but he must have liked my answer,

because he smirked and returned to the boat. He dug through the boat once more for the contraband before giving up his search.

Still not convinced, he returned to the front of the boat and addressed us with his back to the water. And as he talked, our black bag of snacks washed up on shore right behind his feet.

The other boats were getting back into the water to resume the race, but Instructor Stone kept us behind to do push-ups for being in last place. The bag lay directly behind him the entire time.

"Get out of here!" he finally ordered us and walked away. As we pushed our IBS back into the water, I grabbed the bag of goodies and tossed it into the boat.

We lost the next portion of the race, too, because we ate everything that was left inside that bag. That was the only part of our SEAL training where it paid *not* to be a winner.

## TO THE BITTER END

By the time we made it Around the World—or around Coronado Island—the sun was beginning to show itself. It was still dark enough, however, that from a distance we could spot the instructors' signal for us to row our boat ashore: burning coals on the berm in the shape of our class number, 254.

This was it—the final day of Hell Week. It's known as So Sorry Day, although I have never heard a good explanation for the name. And like any other day during Hell Week, on So Sorry Day you have no idea what to expect other than more of the same physical and mental punishment.

It wasn't just the same, as it turned out.

It was worse.

After a short break for a meal—despite the overnight goodies, we were still hungry enough to pack away the calories—it was back into the boats for more races. Then we were sent to the demo (demolition) pit.

The word *pit* doesn't quite provide an adequate description. The pit was about a hundred feet long, about the width of a medium-sized creek—perhaps twenty or twenty-five feet—and about a foot deeper than the tallest trainee was tall. Ordinarily it was empty, but ocean water had been pumped in for Hell Week and allowed to stagnate. Between all the sand and that nasty water, let's just say it's not like a creek you would want to swing out across on a rope and drop into with your friends.

The method for getting into the pit wasn't as much fun as a rope swing either.

When we reached the pit area, we had to begin crawling underneath a long course of barbed wire like we might encounter in combat. On one signal, we crawled forward on our bellies; on a second, we took cover. While we did this crawling/covering up routine, the instructors were creating confusion with blanks-filled machine guns and grenade simulators, as they had at the start of Hell Week. Smoke was piped in over the course, making it difficult to see. And, as always, we were expected to remain with our boat crew or face the consequences. The idea behind this evolution was to create as much commotion as possible and see how we responded, because those were conditions we could easily encounter in a war zone.

Once we made it through the field of barbed wire, we entered the pit through concrete tubes. Those aren't the place for someone who's claustrophobic. They were barely big enough for a man to fit inside, and there was sand and smoke inside them too. The first person through the tubes had to feel his way through and clear out the sand for the others to follow. Then, once we exited the tubes and entered the pit water, the atrocious smell was difficult to take, even after five and a half days of building up our own unique odors.

The demo pit had two ropes extended from one side to the other, with one about six feet higher than the other. Together they formed a makeshift bridge. Each of us had to walk across the lower rope, holding onto the higher rope for balance, while brown shirts stood on each side of the pit and shook the ropes, trying to knock us into the water. If one of our crew members fell in, the rest of us on the team had to jump into the disgusting water and save him. Then the entire team had to start over on trying to cross the pit.

Every evolution during Hell Week had its difficulties, but this one stood out because our sleep-deprived state made our reactions slow, and our weary muscles made our grips on the rope weak. Add in the fact that the brown shirts were fresh and strong and that there was a strong competitive element between them and us, and you get a sense of the intensity involved.

It took a while for all of us to safely cross the pit. On more than one occasion, a team member would have one foot slip off one side of the rope and his other foot slip off the other side, then fall groin-first onto the rope before tumbling down into the pit. Those guys, obviously, were the ones most in need of being rescued from the water.

During the pit evolution, the commotion and lack of sleep got to me. As if those two elements weren't causing enough confusion, instructors kept yelling contradicting orders to test us. One instructor told me to go left, and I was so disoriented that I turned right. He had thrown a grenade simulator to my right into a small concrete pit shaped like a trash can. I looked over into the pit. The instructor screamed, "Get away from there!" but it was too late.

Even though it wasn't a real grenade, it still unleashed a tremendous force when it went off—a flashback to the day the paper towel roll blew up in my face. The fake grenade didn't burn me, of course, but it felt like I got punched in the face. I was so dizzy from the blast that I couldn't stand up right away. I kept trying, but my equilibrium had been rocked, and I kept falling over. The instructor laughed at me and called me an idiot as I tried to get up and then stumbled to the ground.

Early in the afternoon, we were all sent into the demo pit with our backs to the instructors and ordered to duck underwater. We were supposed to stay under for a count of

"One, two, three, hide the trainee!" then lift our heads back above water. But no matter how long we stayed under, it wasn't enough for the instructors. They would call out the name of the first person to emerge from the water and say he came up too early, even if he technically hadn't. Then they would send us right back into the water. We all were holding our breath underwater for as long we could, but someone was always blamed for sending us back down.

Our frustration with each other was growing, and it seemed like we would never be able to satisfy the instructors enough to progress to the next torture they had planned for us, when the order came for an about-face.

When we turned to face the instructors, we saw a US flag with the words, "BUD/S Class 254, congratulations. Hell Week is secured."

## CELEBRATION

It was over. I couldn't believe it. The twenty or so of us who had survived Hell Week were ecstatic. We probably looked like a bunch of Publishers Clearing House sweepstakes winners as we jumped up and down, smiling from ear to ear, slapped each other on the back, and formed a big dog pile. I kept hearing guys shouting things like, "We did it! We did it! I can't believe we did it!" We felt like we had died and arrived in heaven.

We walked to the road to board a bus that would take us back to base for medical checkups. Two wonderful sights greeted us back at the base: pizzas and brown T-shirts. I wolfed down an entire large pepperoni pizza by myself; I don't know that I've ever been more grateful to see a pizza. And I really can't describe how it felt to put on that brown shirt. It's a simple brown T-shirt like you can buy in just about any store. But I could never slip on a shirt that represented more to me than that one shirt.

I had made it. I had persevered through all the cold, the wet, the shivering, the postnap soreness, the broken nose, the instructors' mind games, Brent's departure—everything. This was the biggest accomplishment of my life, and there had never been a doubt along the way that I would make it. I felt invincible, unstoppable. Though more weeks of training lay before me, I could see the end of my road to becoming a SEAL.

I had planned to call Aubrey and my parents as soon as I cleared my medical check. But I was so tired that I crashed into a chair in the common space of our barracks and conked out.

"Williams," an instructor said as he shook me in the chair. He probably had to say my name multiple times to rouse me. "You should probably go to your room now."

So I returned to my room and instantly fell asleep there. I was out cold for I don't know how long. During those two short naps on Wednesday and Thursday, I had awakened to swelling and stiffness. The swelling and stiffness multiplied after that longer sleeping session. My body had started bloating. My fingers were so swollen, they felt like they were going to split. It took every ounce of effort I could muster to even move in my bed. My body was so messed up that I didn't think I could get up to walk to the restroom. None of us could. Instead, we all had empty Gatorade bottles at our beds that we would turn over and urinate into.

When we did need to get up to walk, white shirts from the next BUD/S class helped us get around. They were looking out for us and watching us carefully, and that was much needed and appreciated. The first time I got out of bed to walk downstairs, white shirts helped me make it down the steps.

Weeks before, I had told my mom and dad to make reservations at the Hotel del Coronado for the weekend after Hell Week. On Saturday, my whole family plus Aubrey picked me up at the front gate of the base. Aubrey recalls that I looked horrible, like a bum on the street. I had a scabby bald spot on my head. My face, hands, ankles, and just about anything else you can name were swollen. My eyes were so bloodshot that when I shuffled past people in town, I could hear them say, "Wow, what happened to that guy?"

We got to the luxurious hotel, and I felt really out of place looking all grungy. But it didn't really matter much because I spent most of the time in my room, sleeping. My stay at the hotel was the quickest weekend of my life.

One waking moment I do remember had to do with all the sores, cuts, and scrapes my body had accumulated. The medical staff had advised us to treat them with aloe, so my mom went to a drugstore near the hotel and picked up the only topical aloe medication she could find. But when she applied it to the first cut, I started screaming. It turned out that the aloe medication was mostly alcohol. Needless to say, the rest of my sores, cuts, and scrapes went untreated for the weekend.

Spending that weekend with Aubrey and my family, even if I did sleep most of the time, was one of the most restful and soothing times in my life. It was the calm after the Hell Week storm.

# CHAPTER 8

# ANSWERING THE BELL

*You saw me before I was born. Every day of my
life was recorded in your book. Every moment was
laid out before a single day had passed.*

PSALM 139:16

★　★　★

**THERE IS NO** greater feeling of relief for a SEAL trainee than
to see Hell Week in the rearview mirror. But even after the
completion of our Hell Week, we were nowhere near the end
of our training. We weren't even halfway through First Phase
of BUD/S—with two more phases after that. Over the next
five-plus months of training, we would lose nearly half of
the twenty-some men who had made it through Hell Week.

For me, the next big challenge after Hell Week involved a
bell—but not the quitting bell. It took every ounce of determination I could muster to answer the Monday morning bell
that signaled us to resume training.

My spirit was totally willing. But my flesh could barely
move.

Talk among SEAL circles is that Hell Week takes five years off your life. They also say your body needs a full year to recover completely. I believe that. I had problems with my toes and parts of my feet—mostly numbness—that lasted through the end of Second Phase.

Each class has individuals who are unable to continue after Hell Week because of injuries. Although medical personnel stay busy during the first weeks of BUD/S and Hell Week, many injuries go unreported. Some are relatively minor, like my shin splints, but some determined trainees have been known to keep going despite serious sprains, stress fractures, or even broken bones.

To go to a doctor to have an injury evaluated is to potentially take your SEAL future out of your control. If a doctor pulls you out before or during Hell Week, you might have lost your only chance to become a SEAL. But once you've proved you can make it through Hell Week—*especially* if you continued despite an injury—the Navy has good reason to put you through the rest of the SEAL training, even if you're temporarily unable to continue.

Because of that, it's common for injured trainees to be rolled out of their SEAL class after Hell Week so they can heal and then rejoin BUD/S with a future class. That happened with several members of our class. Likewise, a handful of trainees from previous classes were rolled in to join us after Hell Week. Even more would join us later, especially once we reached Second Phase.

I came close to not being able to continue with our class.

The Monday morning after Hell Week, every part of my body was in agony—except for the toes and parts of my feet that I couldn't feel. Of course, I was more concerned about what I couldn't feel in my feet than about what I could feel from my ankles up.

The first week of conditioning after Hell Week is called Walk Week because walking is about all anyone can do. I could hardly even keep up with that. On top of the pain, I was worried that I would be told, "Hey, you know what? You made it through Hell Week, but maybe we should put you in a rollback."

That was absolutely not in my plan. I had begun my SEAL training with three specific goals. First—and most important—I would die before I quit. Second, I wanted to go through a wintertime Hell Week. And third, I was determined to go straight through the three phases without being rolled out into a later class. So when training resumed, I didn't complain to anyone about my feet or any of the pain I was feeling. No matter what I felt, I was determined to power through. Sure enough, my body did ease back into shape, except for the problems with my feet.

Considering that I'd had about three hours of sleep during the five and a half days of Hell Week, the last thing I expected was that I would encounter problems sleeping afterward. But in the weeks following Hell Week, I couldn't sleep more than an hour or two at a time without waking up drenched in sweat. I also had flashbacks; I would jump out of bed, kicking one leg over like I was in an IBS, and start shouting, "Stroke! Stroke! Stroke!" to the rest of my imaginary crew as though we were in a boat race. I quickly learned not to change my sweat-soaked clothes when this happened because there was a good chance I would repeat that routine and sweat through another set of clothes before waking up for good in the morning.

The Hell Week sweats recurred for several weeks as I gradually progressed to two good hours of sleep, then three, until finally my sleeping was back to normal—four to five hours of sleep per night, which is considered normal during training.

## FINISHING FIRST PHASE

Physical ailments and sleeping problems aside, the final half of First Phase was like running downhill compared to what we had endured the previous weeks. Beginning with that first Monday after Hell Week, I noticed that the instructors seemed to have more respect for us. They took it a little easier on us too. We still had to hit the surf, compete in boat races, complete timed runs, and run the obstacle course. But there were fewer evolutions and fewer exercises following Hell Week, and the emphasis seemed to be more on conditioning than elimination. I think they were trying to help us recover without losing the peak physical condition and the mental toughness we had obtained.

During that time, we learned how to map the bottom of an ocean by making hydrographic charts. The instructors called this skill the bread and butter of SEAL operations. It's basic and old school—the same method the Underwater Demolition Teams (UDTs) employed during World War II, the Korean War, and the Vietnam War when they cleared paths for boats to make amphibious landings. In our era of high technology, it was interesting to learn how our fore-runners had prepared for such missions.

Say, for example, that a reef needed to be charted. The UDT members would use a lead weight and string that was marked in one-foot increments. They would wrap most of the thread around a stick, then lower the weight into the water, spooling out the thread as the weight sank. When they felt it hit bottom, they would note the markings on the thread, say something like, "Okay, seven feet here," and make that designation on a chart.

When we made our hydrographic charts, we had fifteen or so swimmers lined up, covering an area fifty yards wide. They held on to a rope that was pulled tight by guys on each end. Using hand signals, we marked the depth of the ocean floor at intervals. After we had our marks down, we got together, shared all our individual measurements and positions, then used that information to map the ocean floor.

A string and a weight—it was primitive for sure. With today's lasers and computer programs, we can accomplish in minutes what used to take days. But we still devoted a lot of time in the classroom and in the water to learning how to make those hydrographic charts the old-fashioned way. It was an important tradition that gave us an appreciation for the way things used to be, and we could always fall back on those skills if the electronics failed.

The tedious, detailed work really got to us, though. In

fact, we referred to the last week of First Phase, when we were really getting into the nitty-gritty details of mapping, as Hydro Hell Week. It was tough—the Hell Week we didn't know was coming.

Between the classroom and our "lab" in the ocean, we worked on our maps all day and through the night. Attention to detail mattered because maps had to be meticulously perfect. Being off by only one measurement resulted in a complete failure. An accidental scrape on the paper or even the faintest erase mark meant the entire chart was ruined as far as the instructors were concerned. We would spend three or four hours on one chart, and there were times when someone was so tired he nodded off and drew an accidental line across the chart. There went three or four hours of work—just like that—with one slip of his pencil. If we didn't finish one or messed one up, we had to start over, so we became backlogged with beginning a new chart while trying to finish the previous one.

Hydro Hell Week frustrated me because in some ways I felt like I was back in school. On top of that, what we were learning was something we were very unlikely to use in the SEALs because we had electronics that could show us what the bottom of ocean floors looked like. Learning the old-school method was simply a backup—something we could use in emergencies—and a nod to tradition. For me, it was just something else to endure on my way to becoming a SEAL.

At least I was getting closer. The end of hydrographics signaled the end of First Phase. That meant nine weeks down, with four more months to go in BUD/S.

## SECOND PHASE

The good news about Second Phase was that it represented a shift away from the extreme physical training of First Phase. Although we began with another session on the grinder, it was nothing like the one that kicked off BUD/S. We still had our daily timed runs and swims and a little bit of work on the obstacle course, and we still ran those six miles per day to and from chow, but the physical beat-downs were a thing of the past. Our workouts were designed to maintain and finesse our conditioning, not crush us or get us to quit.

The bad news for me was that Second Phase began with a heavy academic load. I had made it through the surf tortures, but now I had to endure classroom tortures! And instead of interacting with the twenty or so brothers I had bonded with, I had to get to know a whole new group of guys. Because of roll-ins from previous classes, our class grew a lot during Second Phase. In fact, the new class members outnumbered those of us remaining from our original class, and that caused a few problems.

There was an almost palpable pride among those of us who had started out with Class 254, made it through Hell Week, and completed First Phase together. At first, we didn't eat with the new guys or have anything to do with them. It took a couple of weeks for us to start getting along, but there was still a line of separation between our original group and the roll-ins.

The best thing about Second Phase was that we finally felt like we were taking part in real-life SEAL activities—like diving. Diving is the main focus of Second Phase, and it was totally new to me. That didn't seem to be a problem. In fact, the instructors actually preferred that I had no experience, because I had no bad habits to break down and correct. Being a diving rookie actually gave me an advantage in learning to dive the SEAL way. So if anyone reading this is considering becoming a SEAL, my strong recommendation is that you do *not* learn to scuba dive beforehand.

Dive training was intense. They say that by the end of Second Phase, SEALs exceed the expertise level of a master diver. Considering we were in the water up to three times every day, I can understand why they say that.

The first two weeks, though, were heavy on classroom learning. We studied dive physics, practiced working with dive tables, and received medical training that helped us understand the biological effects of deep water on divers and learn how to spot and treat symptoms of diving accidents. We had to pass a lot of written tests before we could advance. In First Phase, many trainees dropped out. In the beginning of Second Phase, trainees were just as likely to flunk out.

When we moved from the classroom to the water, we had to demonstrate comfort in the water and the ability to perform our jobs in stressful situations. So while our instructors were no longer in the weeding-out mode, they still put us to the test.

I can't overstate how much emphasis was placed on safety. The type of scuba diving we were learning was safe as long as it was performed correctly, but even the smallest mistake or oversight—particularly in regard to equipment—could create underwater dangers that could prove fatal.

We were required to inspect each other's equipment before diving, then instructors followed to inspect us also. Any safety violation was punished with extra physical training—such as extra push-ups in full scuba gear that could weigh up to 125 pounds. The threat of physical danger combined with the threat of physical training as punishment certainly caused us to pay attention to the safety details.

Our diving lab was what is known as the combat swimmer tank—basically, a glorified swimming pool. We began in the tank with open-circuit rigs, the type of diving equipment that lets air bubbles rise to the surface when you exhale. That stage proved to be a major test that sent guys packing—not because of the diving itself, but because of the "surf hits."

They started once we had demonstrated that we were competent divers. The instructors began putting us in situations of duress to see whether we could handle the pressure without panicking.

For example, the instructors would have us crawl along the bottom of the pool, keeping our eyes down to the floor. They'd wait until a bubble came out to show that we had just exhaled, then they'd "hit" us. They might grab our masks and rip them off—blurring our vision—then pull the mouthpieces from our mouths and tie the mouthpiece tubes in a knot behind our heads. Or they might come up behind us, turn off the air to our two tanks, then turn the "J valve" that connects the two tanks together and opens the air bottles.

Whatever problems the instructors caused with our equipment, we were expected to make corrections according to the procedures that had been outlined in the classroom—all while holding our breath at the bottom of the pool.

Complicating matters was the fact that we never knew when a hit would end. We'd be right in the middle of fixing the equipment when another instructor would sneak up and do something else. The instructors really played up the element of surprise with the surf hits.

Trying to do our emergency repairs without oxygen was a huge challenge. The body begins to fight against itself because it wants to take a breath but can't. The natural inclination is to bolt for the surface. That, however, is very dangerous because ascending too quickly can cause an arterial gas embolism (AGE). With AGE, gas bubbles obstruct the flow of blood, and this can cause damage to major organs, including the brain. It's a common cause of death among scuba divers.

Needless to say, bolting for the surface during a hit was a safety violation that could get us kicked out of training. So the best thing for us to do during the surf hits was to attempt to deal with the problem until we either fixed our equipment or passed out underwater. I never quite reached that point, but others did. They seemed to earn respect from the instructors because they had gone all the way to their last breath without giving up.

There were always divers nearby with what they called octopus rigs, with an extra mouthpiece. They would immediately jam the extra mouthpiece into the mouth of a diver who had passed out and slowly and safely take him to the surface.

At the end of that portion of Second Phase, we were required to take a deep dive off Point Loma. A small group of us and an instructor took a boat out and then dived 120 feet down a descent line. We spent so little time at the bottom that the exercise was called a bounce dive—we just bounced off the bottom and began our ascent. The water was frigid at the bottom near the ocean floor, but at least there weren't any surf hits.

My dive buddy on the bounce dive did experience a "reverse squeeze," which occurs when pressure builds up in the sinuses during the rise to the surface. He either did not or could not clear the squeeze on his way up, and that caused his sinus cavity to burst. Blood began gushing out of his nose so quickly that his face mask filled with blood and he couldn't see. I guided him to the surface, where he removed his mask. I expected that he would be in a lot of pain, but he laughed as soon as the mask was off. "Man," he said, "that hurt until my nose busted." The burst actually gave him relief, and the blood made everything appear much worse than it was.

We wound up with free time after our bounce dive, so we caught lobsters off Point Loma and grilled them on the boat before we came back in. That was a rare opportunity for fun and games during a week of surf hits that knocked out about half of the original members remaining in our class. They had persevered through Hell Week but were simply unable to pass that test.

Fortunately I passed each test on the first attempt. Even though I had never scuba dived, I was comfortable in the water from all my experience surfing and swimming in the ocean growing up. Each time I passed a test, it felt like the weight of the world had been taken off my shoulders.

## SERIOUS DIVING

After the open-circuit rigs, we moved to serious SEAL diving equipment—the Dräger. The Dräger is a German-made "rebreather," a closed-circuit rig that allows a diver to breathe in oxygen and then exhale into a canister that prevents air bubbles from being released and rising. The absence of air bubbles is what allows SEALs to perform underwater combat missions without being detected from the water's surface. By using a Dräger, SEALs can execute a mission requiring as many as four hours underwater.

Unlike basic diving gear, the Dräger attaches in front of the diver. Inside the plastic container is a breathing lung that holds the air the diver will breathe. When a diver breathes, the Dräger's lung contracts. Below the lung is a small oxygen tank.

The Dräger has a right side (the inhalation side) and a left side (the exhalation side). The inhaling side has a check valve that allows air to flow only one way: out. Because of that, when divers exhale, the air can go only into the opposite, or exhalation, side. The exhaled air enters a canister filled with granules that look like cat litter. The granules absorb the carbon dioxide but allow the small amount of oxygen that is exhaled to pass back into the lung to be sent back into the diver's body. That is how the Dräger prevents air bubbles from rising to the surface.

The Dräger can be dangerous if not used correctly. In fact, it is often said that you don't dive the Dräger; you survive it. The rig provides 100 percent oxygen, which sounds like it would be a good thing. But when a combat diver swims deeper into the water, the atmospheric pressure increases, resulting in the oxygen embedding deep within the diver's tissue. This produces various side effects, ranging from a slight tingling sensation or dizziness to uncontrollable convulsions.

Another danger is the "caustic cocktail" that can be created when water gets into the mouthpiece, down the exhaust hose, and into the canister. The resulting toxic gas causes vomiting and, potentially, damage to the esophagus and lungs. To help us recognize the symptoms of this poisoning, we learned an acrostic: VENTID-TC.

**V:** Vision begins to blur
**E:** Ears begin to ring and roar
**N:** Nausea
**T:** Tingling sensations
**I:** Irritability
**D:** Dizziness
**T:** Twitching in face muscles
**C:** Convulsions

Dive partners were on full alert to watch one another for these symptoms. If a partner began convulsing, we knew the tank had become toxic for him and we needed to help him surface.

Even with the dangers, the Dräger is worth using because it gives SEALs a big advantage: secrecy. This is crucial since part of the SEALs' job is underwater demolition, such as setting up explosives under enemy ships or taking out bridges.

Dräger devices were critical aids in the first successful combat swimmer–demolition attack by the US military. As part of the 1989 invasion of Panama, SEALs were called upon to take out a Panamanian patrol boat and a speedboat that Manuel Noriega, the military dictator of Panama, could have used to escape. Two pairs of SEAL divers using the Dräger swam long distances without creating air bubbles, attached explosives to the bottoms of the boats in Balboa Harbor, set the timers, and swam back to a safe distance. The boats were blown to smithereens.

Combat swimmers are used for reconnaissance as well as demolition, and this, too, requires secrecy. Divers rigged with Drägers can enter an enemy harbor undetected, surface next to a pylon under a dock, and execute land surveillance from there. They might even be brought close to the landing site in a submersible SEAL delivery vehicle (SDV). The SDV is flooded, so SEALs inside either breathe from a supply of compressed air in the vehicle or use their diving gear.

SDVs can be anchored underwater so that SEALs can exit to perform missions at sea or on land. It's funny to consider, but SEALs doing surveillance from a mountaintop would have secretly arrived to the area underwater.

## NAVIGATING UNDERWATER

Our training in Second Phase involved more than just diving equipment, of course. We also learned how to find our way underwater with a tack-board that included a compass. GPSes can often be used underwater to measure distance traveled, but we learned the old-school way for when GPS was unavailable or unusable.

We trained in pairs, with our swim buddies. The diver with the tackboard was the navigator. The other diver would be constantly on the lookout for obstacles. Believe it or not, there are all kinds of objects underwater, especially closer to shore, that divers can bump their heads against.

Once we proved adept at a particular exercise in daytime, we would then perform the same exercise at night, because that is when most SEAL underwater combat missions are carried out. SEALs wear all black and paint any exposed skin dark for nighttime underwater missions. The brightest thing a diver might wear is an LED on a watch, and at the depths SEALs swim, that would not be detectable from the surface.

An important part of our training was learning how many kicks of our feet would take us specified distances. That, too, is part of the traditional way of measuring distances.

Kicks vary from swimmer to swimmer. One swim pair might cover 100 yards in 100 kicks, while another might require 125 kicks. Each pair knew its kicks, and we would count the kicks as we swam in order to calculate distance while the navigator used the compass on the tackboard for bearing. We also had to factor in the current, so it was essential that we knew what the tide was doing when we swam and how that would affect us.

In other words, every dive involved a fair amount of underwater math. When we knew the distance we would have to swim, we would determine, "We're going to have to go at this bearing for eight hundred kicks, then turn and swim another bearing for nine hundred kicks."

We practiced these types of missions all the time. If all went well, we would kick for an hour and a half or so and then, at the predetermined kick count, think, *Okay, we should be there right now.*

One of the many cool things about being underwater is that even at night there are shadows. It was a great sign when we reached our kick count and realized the water was darker there than it had been. That darker shadow meant a boat was above us.

We would slowly rise toward the surface. Underwater identification marks would tell us whether we had reached our assigned boat. If so, we attached a fake limpet mine to the bottom of the boat and dove back out. If an instructor spotted us at any point, we failed that evolution. We had to pass a number of evolutions to make it through Second Phase.

I loved that phase once we got out of the classroom. I was comfortable and performed well in the water, and what we were learning gave me my first taste of what it would feel like to be a SEAL.

# CHAPTER 9

# FINALLY—A SEAL!

*I am certain that God, who began the good work*
*within you, will continue his work until it is finally*
*finished on the day when Christ Jesus returns.*

PHILIPPIANS 1:6

★    ★    ★

"FUN'S OVER."

That's how the classroom instructor introduced us to Third Phase.

"You guys have had an easy couple of months, just diving in the water," he continued. "Now it's time to get serious and start learning how to use deadly stuff."

I'd already realized we had a lot of learning ahead because we had yet to pick up a weapon. Still, entering Third Phase made us feel like we were putting on some big-boy clothes.

We'd spent two entire months becoming top-notch divers, but there was a lot more to pack into our final two months of BUD/S: land navigation, land warfare, and underwater and out-of-water demolition. Because we were SEALs in the making, we wouldn't merely learn. We would become experts.

We started with land navigation. My training sessions with Scott had exposed that as a weakness of mine, and I continued to struggle in that area. I had a tendency to get disoriented easily, and that made for some of my most stressful experiences in BUD/S training.

For our land-navigation evolutions, we would be allotted eight hours to find our way around certain courses and hit a specific number of geographic points, all while toting fifty to eighty pounds of gear on our backs. It seemed I almost always came down to the final, nerve-racking thirty minutes before completing the assignments. Most of the time, a slight error would create a ripple effect that set me off course. Then I had to scramble to recover.

My stubbornness added to my problems.

We had been taught very basic navigation techniques, such as how to use a compass and how to understand an eight-digit grid on a map. An eight-digit grid narrows a location to within ten meters of a target. If we became lost, our training was intended to help us determine our location.

In the Laguna Mountains, where some of our training took place, for example, I should have been able to figure out where I was by taking a bearing of a specific mountaintop, marking it on the map, using a ruler to draw the opposite of that bearing back to where I was, then pointing out another mountaintop and drawing back to where the points intersected on my map. There was step-counting involved too.

I know that probably sounds confusing. Using that method involves quite a few measurements, but the technique is actually pretty simple and effective for most people. Many instructors recommended it for beginners. "Baby steps," they called it.

But I've never been a detail person, and I wasn't interested in baby steps. So I went for the more advanced method the instructors taught us, one that involved understanding the contours of a map so we could walk around and work things out merely by orientation. SEAL teams that follow the second method typically have a GPS device with them. I didn't have a GPS, but I was still determined to use that method. No wonder I struggled.

I made it through the evolutions by the skin of my teeth almost every time, barely passing land navigation. Another handful of guys from our original class didn't pass. They had to go before a board that determined whether each would be dropped from training entirely or would receive another chance in a later class. So we lost a few more guys during that part of our training.

## BACK TO "THE ROCK"

After land navigation, we moved to Camp Pendleton to begin weapons training. We not only needed to become proficient in shooting various weapons, but we also had to know our weapons, be able to assemble and disassemble them, and thoroughly understand weapons safety.

My only exposure to guns before Third Phase had consisted of one visit with Scott to a shooting range and an introductory session at boot camp. As with scuba diving, that wasn't a negative, because I went into weapons training without any bad habits to correct.

The daily physical evolutions at Camp Pendleton were some of the most difficult we'd encountered since Hell Week. We had to complete eight-mile runs carrying our gear, equipment, and weapons and take turns carrying a seventy-five-pound log for two minutes each. While we ran, instructors watched us closely for safety violations with our weapons. A violation, as usual, led to extra physical training.

One of our final assignments at Camp Pendleton turned out to be one of the most difficult runs of the entire BUD/S process. It was pouring rain, and each of us had to run with a fifty-pound, sand-filled rucksack on his back. The steel frame of the rucksack rubbed the skin of my back raw. I still have dark scars from that run that cause people to ask, "What happened to your back?"

After that final run, it was off to San Clemente Island for the remainder of Third Phase. My first stay on that island, waiting for my BUD/S class to begin, had almost been a vacation. My second trip to "the Rock" was all business.

On San Clemente we fired hundreds and thousands of rounds per day with the M4, our basic rifle. We were always being graded, and there were established scores we had to attain, so there was constant pressure to perform well.

We learned how to transition from our rifle to a handgun and from a handgun back to the rifle. Such transitions were why we spent so much time shooting at targets—developing muscle memory. We also learned how to problem-solve when our rifles didn't fire. We followed a procedure called "tap-rack-bang."

If we pulled the trigger and the rifle clicked, the first thing we had to do was tap it, or jam the magazine into the rifle to make sure it was properly inserted. If that didn't work we would rack, or check for a bad round, then fire the rifle again. If the rifle still didn't fire, we would have to drop the magazine out of the rifle, rack the rifle chamber, look inside the rifle to make sure it was clear, check the magazine, then jam the magazine back into the rifle and drive the bolt forward to chamber a new round for another pull of the trigger. All this had to be performed rapidly, without even thinking, so we could do it in a combat situation, such as when we were working our way through a building and a person we didn't know ran toward us. Our lives could depend on a rapid tap-rack-bang.

Explosives were the next focus of our training. C-4 was our charge of choice. It has 1.34 times the power of dynamite, so every pound of C-4 used in an explosion provides the equivalent of 1.34 pounds of dynamite (quite a bit more power than fifteen gutted model-rocket engines).

We were taught about the different kinds of charges we could set and when to use them. We learned how to use blasting caps and detonation cords with the C-4. We also practiced setting those charges underwater, so all that underwater knot tying we'd done in the previous two phases came in handy after all.

For me, one of the most fascinating aspects of explosives training was learning how to shape charges. Even though a blast happens fast, its elements can be broken down into steps, and each step is delicately planned. For instance, the direction at which a blasting cap is placed in a charge determines how a blast will go. The shaped charges we used acted much like rocket-propelled grenades (RPGs). When an RPG hits a tank or a Humvee, it isn't the actual shrapnel that kills those inside. The shrapnel is basically at the tail end of the blast. It is the overpressure ahead of the molten-hot slug of shrapnel that kills.

It really is as cool as it sounds to set off a five-hundred-pound charge of C-4 underwater. But even better than that—unofficially, of course—was the time I set off a five-hundred-pound charge underwater that accidentally detonated a *second* five-hundred-pound charge we had set up.

The power of the blasts was awesome. We could literally feel the earth shake from our safe distance. The force of both charges sent water, part of the ocean floor, and concrete and steel from underwater obstacles soaring more than a hundred feet into the air. I don't think any marine life in the blast zone survived. There were fish floating on the surface, providing a feast for a flock of seagulls that happened to be in the right place at the right time.

## SHARKS!

Ocean swims, both daytime and nighttime, were part of our routine at San Clemente Island. One swim especially stands out in my memory. It was our longest swim—5 nautical miles, or about 5.75 standard miles.

When I was on the island before BUD/S, in my white-shirt days, I had earned a reputation among the instructors because of my work as a deckhand on sport-fishing boats. The instructors would go out in their boats and come back with nice catches of yellowtail, albacore, and bluefin. Because of my deckhand skills, I was appointed to fillet and package the instructors' catches. That earned me the nickname of Ginsu Master.

When we prepared to head out to the island for Third Phase, therefore, the instructors ordered me to add an extra "weapon" to the assault gear I always carried with me: a fourteen-inch fillet knife.

I enjoyed filleting fish to begin with, and doing so on the island provided welcome, mind-numbing relaxation for me. More important, I was secretly awarded a fifteen-minute call home at the end of each week in exchange for filleting instructors' fish. We weren't allowed to make calls from the island, so that fifteen-minute connection to home meant a lot.

My position as Ginsu Master also wound up saving me from a particularly scary experience.

When I filleted the instructors' fish, I threw the fish remains into a white bucket. Then I hauled the bucket to the beach and dumped the contents into the surf. One night, though, as I was finishing my routine, an instructor came up to me.

"Ginsu Master, I want you to save that white bucket of junk this time and leave it where it is. Don't throw it out."

"Hoo-yah!" I responded.

The next morning that white bucket was gone. The next time I saw it was a week later, before the start of our longest swim.

The instructors gathered us at five o'clock that morning for a classroom presentation—complete with PowerPoint slides and video clips—about shark attacks. Then they informed us that San Clemente Island was a breeding ground for all kinds of sharks, including great whites. From my experience fishing those waters, I knew the instructors weren't pulling our legs.

When the classroom session ended, we lined up in ranks outside before heading to the water. The sun wasn't up yet, so it was still pretty dark. As an instructor began to give us our orders, I saw the white bucket beside him.

"Give me ten volunteers!" the instructor ordered.

Usually I tried to be one of the first to run forward when the instructors asked for volunteers, but after spotting that bucket I knew better. Ten guys ran forward and, as ordered, dropped to the ground. I guessed what was coming next.

The instructor picked up the bucket and began pouring week-old fish blood and guts all over those poor, helpless souls. After being fully educated about shark attacks, those guys had just had shark bait dumped on them. And now they were preparing to enter the water.

One of the toughest guys in our class, Bates, came up to me before we entered the water.

"You used to work on fishing boats. We don't really have anything to worry about, right?"

I had to tell him the truth. "Bates, I wish I could tell you that. But you see that cove out there?"

"Yeah."

"That's where the boat I used to work on anchored up overnight to cut our fish. Usually within fifteen minutes of throwing that stuff in the water—that same stuff that was just poured over you—we'd have sharks swimming around our boat."

Bates's eyes grew large with shock and fear. His face turned as white as a ghost.

The twisted part of me at that time in my life caused me to add, "Just stay away from me when we get in the water." Then I turned and walked away.

By the grace of God, I'm sure, no one was attacked by sharks on that swim, and to this day I'm still baffled as to why not.

My swim buddy, however, did get attacked by a sea lion during that swim. That was actually quite humorous. The sea lion must have sensed fear in my buddy because he never came after me. Instead, the sea lion kept ramming and biting at my buddy's fins. Even though my friend had his knife in his hand, somehow he couldn't manage to stab anything

·other than some seaweed! Luckily, the only wounds he suffered that day were isolated to his ego.

## GOOD-BYE TO BUD/S

By the time we left San Clemente Island, we were experts at demolition and at shooting handguns and rifles. We would soon learn that we weren't quite as proficient as we believed we were, but our training had made us experts compared to the rest of the military. Even better, we were finished with BUD/S.

Forty-six of us graduated from BUD/S Class 254. About thirty had been rolled in at various points after Hell Week. Of the 173 who had first showed up to be a part of BUD/S Class 254, only thirteen had made it to this point.

But we weren't SEALs yet.

The big graduation celebration was saved for after completion of Jump School (for the "Air" part of SEAL) and SQT, or Seal Qualification Training. Once I had graduated from BUD/S, though, I felt like my foot was in the door.

I had about four weeks off between BUD/S graduation and reporting to Jump School at the Army's Fort Benning in Georgia. My on-again, off-again relationship with Aubrey was in one of its off periods, so I spent much of my time hanging out again with my high school friends and guys from the community.

I had turned twenty-one during Third Phase and was finally legal for the club scene. Able to get into the clubs without sneaking past a security guard and not needing to rely on someone to purchase alcohol for me, I could really get rowdy, and I did.

During boot camp I had stayed away from alcohol. At A-School (sailor training) I might have had a couple of drinks. I stopped drinking entirely when BUD/S started and only drank occasionally after making it through Hell Week. Now, during my leave time after BUD/S, I started drinking heavily.

In addition to club hopping, I went out on cocktail cruises with a friend who had a boat in the harbor. We would invite friends to go out drinking with us, and we were always trying to come up with something crazy to do. We got a kick out of diving off the boat in the middle of the night, then sneaking back and scaring our friends who were still in the boat.

During that time I occasionally drank enough to have blackouts. It was like entering a time warp. I'd wake up somewhere at six in the morning, and the last thing I'd remember was sitting at my parents' kitchen table the evening before. I wouldn't be able to recall anything that had happened during that time period.

But even with the blackouts, I still didn't experience hangovers. I never felt a sense that what I was doing could mess up my body.

In fact, there had been one weekend at home during BUD/S when I stayed out late drinking sake bombs before returning to Coronado. I grabbed a couple of hours of sleep at home, then left at four-thirty in the morning to return to the base. I was pretty buzzed when I showed up at six o'clock for a four-mile timed run, laughing with the guys and telling them about my night out. The guys were worried about my condition for the run. I still smelled like alcohol, and they were concerned about what the instructors might do to me. But I finished second place in that run, with one of the best times I ever recorded. Once again, I hadn't suffered any consequences for my drinking, so there was no reason to stop.

## THE REST OF MY TRAINING

Once my post-BUD/S leave ended and I left home and the party scene, the rest of SEAL training went well and, fortunately, was mostly uneventful.

Jump School was pretty basic, starting with static-line jumping, in which everyone lined up in an airplane with a lanyard hooked to a cable that was part of the plane. We ran and jumped out of the back of the plane, and the static line automatically opened our parachutes for us. Those were round parachutes that we did not have much control over. From there, we progressed to free-falling and more advanced parachutes that we learned how to control so that during combat we could land in an exact spot in a combat zone or in enemy territory.

SQT was where we learned that we weren't quite the experts we'd thought we were coming out of BUD/S. SQT is advanced SEAL training. It involves taking the skills acquired in Second Phase and Third Phase and raising them to a whole new level for use in combat. The learning curve was even steeper than it had been during BUD/S, as we were now taught advanced techniques in diving, swimming, and land warfare.

SQT included a trip to Kodiak Island in Alaska for cold-weather training, especially in land navigation. Not only would I struggle to find my direction, but I would do so while shivering! The Alaskan weather made me wish I were more adept at land navigation so I could get out of the cold sooner.

As part of our SQT weapons instruction, we learned to shoot and move in the desert and communicate with others in the platoon. When we learned how to conduct direct assaults in close quarters—like a house—we actually used real ammunition around our buddies. At that stage, the instructors were loosening their reins on us a little to see how fast we could master the advanced techniques.

Where before we had been crawling as SEALs—although we didn't realize that at the time—now we were walking and even running.

After completing SQT, we were considered ready to deploy for combat. In other words, almost twenty months after leaving for boot camp, on December 9, 2005, I became a Navy SEAL!

# CHAPTER 10

# THE NIGHT EVERYTHING CHANGED

*I will give them singleness of heart and put a new spirit*
*within them. I will take away their stony, stubborn*
*heart and give them a tender, responsive heart.*

EZEKIEL 11:19

★   ★   ★

*ALL RIGHT, SCOTT, we made it!* I thought when the Navy
SEAL trident was pinned onto the left chest of my uniform
for the first time.

All the work, all the physical and mental persever-
ance—the shivering in the Pacific Ocean and sweating on
the grinder, the scrambling to find my way in the Laguna
Mountains and Alaska—it had all led to that moment when I
received the insignia that let everyone who saw it know I was
officially a SEAL. I had done what I said I would do. I had
accomplished my "big thing."

My limit of twenty family members and friends drove
down for the graduation ceremony to share with me one

of the happiest days of my life. Then we all headed up to Huntington Beach, where my parents had planned a big graduation party for me at home. I drove alone in my truck, with plenty of time to reflect on what had just taken place.

That trip home became one of the saddest times of my life.

The farther I drove and the deeper I reflected, the more let down I felt. I had reached my mountaintop, only to discover after a brief look around that the view disappointed me. And there was no higher step to take. I had reached as high as I could reach, accomplished everything I believed I could accomplish.

*I just graduated two hours ago, and this is how I feel?*

My entire focus had been on making it through the rigorous process of becoming a SEAL. Now that I had done that, what else was there?

I still wanted to be a SEAL. I still wanted to serve my country overseas. I still carried my motivation from Scott's death. But even with all that, I just couldn't see how anything about being a SEAL could take me any higher than what I had achieved to become a SEAL.

There had to be more than a hundred people at my parents' house for the celebration. Everywhere I turned, someone was walking up to me with a "Congratulations, Chad!"

"Thanks," I would answer with a smile—a fake smile. I knew they expected me to appear excited, but deep down I wasn't. Why did I feel so disappointed?

I was confused. It didn't make sense to feel this way, but

I did. This was what I had been building toward, and now that I was here, something was missing. I just couldn't identify what it was.

I didn't tell anyone how I felt. I just began looking around for the missing piece. Unfortunately, I started my search in all the wrong places. I decided I could make myself feel better by embracing a thrill-seeking life.

*I'm going to live like a rock star!* I told myself. *I'm going to see it all, do it all—live big the way a SEAL should.* That is when I reached a new level of recklessness—not only with my drinking, but with my entire lifestyle.

## LIVING RECKLESSLY

Upon graduation, I had been assigned to immediately report to SEAL Team 1, which had just come off a mission and would be going through another year-and-a-half training cycle before its next deployment.

There are nine SEAL teams, numbered 1 to 8 and 10. The odd-numbered teams are based on the West Coast, at Coronado, and the even-numbered teams are based in Virginia. At any given time, two of the nine SEAL teams will be forward deployed—one a West Coast team, the other an East Coast team.

What many people do not know is that a SEAL team consists of multiple platoons, not just one. A team usually will have three task units, and each task unit will be broken down into two platoons, with approximately sixteen SEALs in each platoon. That is ninety-six SEALs, plus probably a couple dozen more in leadership positions. So about 100 to 120 SEALs comprise one team. When a team is deployed, its six platoons will be sent to places all over the world—to obvious war zones like Iraq and Afghanistan and to other places, areas where the public does not know a SEAL presence exists.

I was glad I had landed on a West Coast team. That meant I'd be able to see my family and Aubrey often. (Aubrey and I were "on" again.) It also meant I could maintain my high-octane partying with both my old friends and my new SEAL buddies. I threw a lot of energy into doing just that.

After one weekend trip home, I decided to drive the motorcycle I had bought back to my team. San Diego is 110 miles from home, and it took me less than an hour to make the trip. Why did I drive that fast? For the thrill, I guess. That's how recklessly I began living. I was careless with my life and careless with others' lives. As far as I was concerned, anyone who didn't want to be a part of my thrill-seeking was a sissy.

During off-hours, with my SEAL team, I would do anything the established SEALs wanted me to do. I was young, I was impressionable, and I had no fear of pushing the envelope with everything I did. When members of the team wanted me to drive them to a bar, I was happy to do it. Then I would drink inside with them and drive us back to the base. If one of the guys on the team wound up in a fight, I would jump right in.

I showed equally poor judgment when I came home to Huntington Beach. I wasn't above flaunting my status as a SEAL, even though we weren't supposed to do that. If my friends and I were at the back of a line at the bar, a buddy would say, "My friend's a SEAL! Let us up front!" That worked, and we would zoom up to the front of the line. Often a total stranger would step forward to pay for my drinks.

There were times, though, when someone in a bar would want to size me up and try to test me physically. So I would go outside with him and prove that I indeed was a SEAL. A few times the police were called, and I had to take off running. But I knew they'd never catch me—not on foot, anyway. My only concern was the possibility of a police helicopter locking in on me from above. But that never happened, and they never came close to apprehending me. I hid in people's backyards. I opened unlocked cars and hid inside. I knew downtown Huntington Beach like the back of my hand and knew how to work my way around the side streets and alleys.

I could always get away, so I had no reason to avoid trouble. I didn't even try.

One night I took care of three guys at once on the streets. I thought nothing of taking on those "regular" people. I was a trained SEAL, and I knew I could mow through them like they were nothing.

I wouldn't start the fights, but when some guy wanted to prove he was tougher than me, I didn't back down. My friends would instigate fights, too, then bring me into them. And I always covered for my friends.

## ON THE RUN

All this time, I believed in a twisted theology that told me I could live the way I was living and still be in good standing with God as long as I had "a good heart." And my definition of having a good heart was pretty broad. It basically meant I had some good intentions. I could end up with someone else's blood on my shirt after a fight, and if I was concerned about the guy I had just beaten up—if I thought, *I hope he's okay*—that meant I had a good heart and I would go to heaven when I died.

I'm not kidding; I really did think that way. And I wasn't shy about spreading my theology in bars and clubs. "Hey," I would tell someone, "all that matters is that you have a good heart, because God knows our hearts."

One time I encountered a group of guys handing out gospel tracts on a street corner in Huntington Beach. I looked at them as an embarrassment. An embarrassment to whom, I don't know, but that's the way I felt about them. One of them tried to hand me a tract while I was on my way to a bar, and I shoved him aside. "You're going too far with it," I told him. "You don't need to do all that kind of stuff."

Then I proceeded into the bar, where I attempted to justify my shove by espousing my theology of "All that matters is that we each have a good heart."

As if a person with a good heart would needlessly shove another person who was politely passing out tracts.

That was my version of Christianity, and I really thought I was all right with God because I always seemed to come out on top no matter what kind of trouble I caused or stepped into. That added to my already overinflated sense of invincibility. I was convinced that God had my back and wouldn't allow anything bad to happen to me. No matter how dire a situation I might put myself in, I thought the combination of my muscles, my mind, and God would get me off the hook every time.

That attitude was exemplified one early, early morning when I was walking around Huntington Beach after visiting local bars. All the bars had closed by two thirty, but I wasn't ready to go home, so I just kind of moseyed around downtown. I was one of the only people on the streets at that hour, walking along the Pacific Coast Highway near Main Street. My walk must have been a little wobbly, because I caught the attention of a couple of policemen. I was also barefoot because at some point during the night, I had lost my sandals. I was always losing my sandals for some reason.

The cops and I made eye contact with each other. I knew the meaning of the looks in their eyes.

*Uh-oh*, I thought.

"Hey, stop!" they called out to me after I walked past them.

I turned and stopped long enough to think, *I could get a public intoxication right now, or I could just run.*

"Come here," one of the officers told me.

*You're going to have to catch me first*, I thought as I quickly decided to make a run for the pier.

There were hardly any cars out at that time of morning,

and I darted across the Pacific Coast Highway with the officers starting their pursuit.

There is a fence with a locked gate at the pier when it is closed for the night. But I had scaled fences with eighty pounds of gear during SEAL training, so climbing that fence in street clothes—even barefoot—was a piece of cake. My heart was racing, not from fear of being caught but from the thrill of the chase.

The closest the policemen came to me was while I was climbing the fence. Once I cleared the fence, I knew I had it made. The pier was well lit and empty.

The officers climbed the fence and chased after me down the pier, though they were a good distance behind me. I knew exactly where I was headed, and as I raced toward the end, I felt like an airplane about to take off from a runway.

I hadn't jumped off the pier since that day with Brent, and I had been warned then that if I got caught doing so again, the consequences would be more severe than that $110 fine. But this time I didn't have to worry about Brent slowing me down. So I sprinted to the end of the pier and jumped.

In the water, I decided to execute a maneuver we had learned in Second Phase—a box dive. I figured the cops would expect me to swim directly back toward shore. So instead I followed a box pattern—I swam out to sea first, then swam over for a little bit before turning back toward the beach. I was comfortable in the water and laughed out loud a few times before reaching the shore probably a half mile from the pier.

There was no sign of the police, or anyone else for that matter. I assumed, though, that the cops would still be looking for me. I was a long way from home, and my cell phone was soaked and unusable. So I decided to work my way through the alleys toward home. Along the way, I came across an unlocked van. I hopped in and sat in a seat in the back to relax for a while. The next thing I knew, I was waking up to sunshine and the sounds of chirping birds and lawn mowers.

It took me a few minutes to get my bearings. My clothes were still wet, and I was sitting inside a van I didn't recognize. As I looked around, I began to recall what had led me to this spot. That got me pumped up again.

*Whoa! Yeah, man! Oh, yeah!*

Then I wondered, *Who picked me up?*

I opened the glove compartment to see if there were any documents bearing the owner's name. I didn't recognize the name.

Then I started to freak out.

*Oh, man. Oh, man. This is completely illegal.*

(As if being drunk in public and running from the cops hadn't been illegal too.)

I got out of the van and looked around to figure out where I was. I actually had to walk over about a block to find a street name I recognized. I was still a good ways from home.

I started my walk, passing people on their morning walks and jogs. I was still wet and barefoot, and I was walking on the ends of my jeans as they hung over my feet. I got some strange looks on my way home, and I'm sure I did look like a freak.

My parents had become accustomed to my coming home at three or four in the morning, although they let me know they didn't like that. But this time it was closer to seven o'clock. I didn't have my keys on me. Typically, in that situation I would climb up to a second-floor window and enter there. But that morning I didn't feel like climbing, so I knocked on the door.

My mom answered with tears in her eyes. "Where have you been?"

"I just had the time of my life!" I told her.

She went from moist eyes to all-out crying, and I think I said a foul word to her, being shamefully disrespectful.

I walked past her and upstairs to my room to fall asleep.

There was another night when a friend picked a fight that I finished, whipping three guys. That was one of the instances when I was proud of myself for hoping someone I had beaten up was okay. My shirt had been ripped off in the fight, and I had someone else's blood all over me when I knocked on our door.

Mom started crying again when she answered and saw me shirtless and covered in blood.

"What have you been doing?" she asked. "Where are you cut?"

I walked right past her without answering. What she said as I walked past didn't faze me then, but it stings now:

"What are you turning into?"

One night, though, did come as close to a wake-up call as I probably could have experienced at that stage of my life.

It was one of those nights when I blacked out after drinking. The first moment I remember was sitting in the back of the car wrapped in a blanket, with Dad driving and Mom in the passenger seat. Mom was crying—I made her cry way too much—and Dad was visibly upset, even shaking a little as best as I can remember.

"What are you guys doing?" I asked.

"We're driving you to your SEAL team," Dad answered. "You have to be there."

I pulled my arms out from under the blanket and saw that a knuckle on my right hand was cut wide open.

"You need help," my dad said.

I said something about my knuckle, and Dad said I had somehow gashed my finger and been spreading blood from the knuckle all over the walls of the house. And that I had threatened my sister Melissa. And that I had tried to fight Dad in the garage.

When Dad said that, I had a flashback of standing face-to-face with him in the garage and shouting that I was going to rip his head off.

I didn't know what to think, but that's how out of control my life had become.

Dad and Mom dropped me off at the base. "What did you do?" a guy on our team asked when he saw my hand.

"I don't know," I said and laughed, proud that I was still drunk.

"That's not funny," the guy snapped. "Go over to Medical. Get that stitched up."

*Man*, I thought, *what's his deal? I do anything these guys want me to do. I thought he'd be proud of me. I'm living like a SEAL!*

At Medical, twenty-six stitches were needed to close the cut.

## GOING OFF SCRIPT

The next weekend I returned home, ready for more drinking and partying.

"We have to talk," my dad told me.

It was back to my parents' bedroom, the scene of so many "Chad's in trouble again" talks.

"We can't have you stay here anymore if you're going to keep going out and doing these things," Dad said.

"You're taking years off our lives," Mom added.

"We love you," Dad went on, "but we can't just harbor you at this house. If you're going to be like that, you need to stay somewhere else. We can't do this anymore."

I became furious.

"You're my family!" I screamed at both of them. "How could you do this? I'll find somewhere else to stay, but I can't believe you won't let me stay here!"

To be honest, I hadn't been using their house as anything more than a bed when I came home for weekends. I didn't spend time with my family. I went out drinking with my friends, stumbled home early in the morning, went straight to my bedroom to sleep, then woke up to go drinking again. Why should they have supported that? Of course, that wasn't my thinking then.

I knew I could easily find a friend to stay with when I came home, but I did have one problem that needed an immediate solution. I had a keg, hidden under a blanket in the garage, that I planned to use that night. Dad and Mom seemed pretty serious about kicking me out right away, so how could I get to that keg?

I had to buy some more time at their house.

"Hey," I said to them. "You guys are going to some church thing tonight, aren't you?"

"Yeah," they responded, obviously wondering where that was headed.

"I'll go with you."

Shock covered their faces. I had rarely gone to church with them in the past several years when they'd asked, much less offered to go on my own.

"You will?" they asked.

"Yeah," I confirmed, still kind of buying into the idea myself.

My intentions were completely disingenuous, but I did have a plan. I knew the church service would end around nine o'clock, or ten at the latest. My night wouldn't begin until sometime between eleven and midnight. Going to church with my parents would probably buy me one more night at home. And I would be back in plenty of time to get the keg and leave for the party.

I called Aubrey to fill her in on what was up and tell her that I wanted her to go to the service with us. I also gave her a heads-up about what to expect at church.

"Look, this is what we're going to do. We're going to this church thing tonight, and from what I understand it's kind of a special deal—a crusade. They're having it outside the church, underneath this big tent."

Aubrey had grown up Roman Catholic, but I don't think her family attended Mass often. Based on my experiences in churches growing up, I felt like I needed to caution her about what would take place. I considered it all a little strange myself, and I didn't want Aubrey to get too freaked out.

"When we get there," I told her, "there's going to be people playing music up on stage. People will be clapping, and they'll know the words to the songs that you haven't heard, and they'll be singing along to it. And then there's this guy named Greg Laurie—I've heard him speak before, and he's actually a pretty cool dude. He'll share a message about God, and then he'll basically ask everyone in the audience to respond in a certain way if the message has affected them. Something like, 'If you want to get right with God, just raise your hand where you are.'"

I was careful to warn Aubrey, "Do *not* raise your hand. If you raise your hand, he's going to ask you to stand up. But it's a trick. Because once you stand up, he's going to get you to walk down to the front. Then once you're up front, they'll take you into a back room where someone will talk to you. Then they'll give you some things. And we don't have time for all that, because we have somewhere else to go afterward."

I summarized for her my three points: "There's going to be some music. Greg Laurie will get up and talk. And don't raise your hand."

There had to be at least a thousand people under the tent when the service began, and the script followed exactly what I had told Aubrey would happen. At one point during the singing, I gave Aubrey a told-you-so look. She gave me her sweet little smile. She was doing exactly as I had advised. My parents were pleased I was there, so everything was going perfectly according to *my* script too.

*Just a little longer, and we'll be able to get out of here and go to our party.*

When the message began, I was kind of numb to what was being said. I felt like I was seeing right through what the speaker was up to. I could tell where everything was headed—as I had told Aubrey—and knew without a doubt that he was going to try to trick people into coming down to the front later.

But if you have heard Greg Laurie, the widely known senior pastor of Harvest Christian Fellowship in Riverside, California, you know what an engaging speaker he is. He has such a down-to-earth personality that it's difficult to listen to him speak without actually hearing what he's saying.

Gradually, I started paying more attention to his message. He was talking about this guy named Naaman from the Old Testament. I had never heard of Naaman, but he was someone I could relate to. The man was the successful commander of an army—he was a soldier—and he had an interesting story.[1] Naaman was revered by his men and had a lot of power. But Naaman also had a problem: leprosy.

So here was this big, powerful man with his body covered by armor. His body was likely covered by leprosy, too, but no one could see it because of his armor. As Laurie continued to describe Naaman's situation, I could picture this strong, impressive man whose flesh was gradually rotting away.

Naaman heard about a prophet named Elisha who could potentially take the leprosy away from him, so Naaman and his men decided to pay Elisha a visit.

I was totally into the story now.

Naaman and his servants went to Elisha's house, but Elisha wouldn't even pay him the courtesy of meeting him at the door. Instead, Elisha sent a messenger to talk to the commander. "Go to the river," the messenger told Naaman, "and dip yourself in the water seven times."

It ticked Naaman off that the prophet hadn't come out and healed him. It ticked me off too, because I was now imagining what it would be like to be Naaman.

*Why won't this prophet of God talk to him and heal him?*

I was sitting forward in my seat, wondering what would happen to my new friend, Naaman. Aubrey was to my right, but I had no idea whether she was getting into the story too, because I had tunnel vision. My eyes were locked directly in on Pastor Laurie on the stage.

Even though Naaman was upset, his servants convinced him that he had nothing to lose by dipping in the river as Elisha had prescribed through the messenger.

Pastor Laurie described how it must have felt for Naaman—big, strong, powerful military leader Naaman—to have to strip off his armor and, perhaps for the first time, allow the people who revered him to see the sores on his skin.

I imagined how shocked Naaman's servants would have been and the total humiliation he would have experienced.

But still, Naaman decided to dip into the river. He dipped once and nothing happened. He did it a second time and still nothing happened.

*Was Naaman feeling like a fool? I would be.*

Then came a third time, and a fourth, and so on until Naaman finally walked into the river for the seventh time. When he came out of the water that last time, all the leprosy had disappeared. His skin immediately had become as clear as anyone could want. As smooth as a baby's skin.

Then I remembered that at the beginning of the sermon, Pastor Laurie had brought his baby granddaughter, Stella, on stage, showed her off to the audience, and pointed out how smooth her skin was.

Now Naaman's leprosy-infested skin, which I had pictured in my mind, was as smooth as the skin of Pastor Laurie's baby granddaughter.

At about this point, it seemed as though Pastor Laurie stopped telling a story to a thousand people and started relating it one-on-one to me.

Sin, he said, is a lot like the leprosy Naaman suffered from in that it causes decay.

"Maybe you're a person," he continued, "who puts on this tough, outer shell, but inside you know things aren't right."

*Man, he is talking to me.*

A sense of conviction immediately came over every square inch of my body. It was different from anything I had ever felt.

Remember, I had never felt bad about my drinking.

I might have felt just a little bad for beating up certain people and hoped they turned out okay, but I hadn't let it bother me that much.

I hadn't even felt bad about tricking my parents earlier that evening and going to church with them as a way to keep access to that keg.

But now, all of a sudden, a door seemed to open in my soul, and I began to feel so sorry for a list of things running through my mind—things I had done wrong. Along with that came a sense of urgency, a feeling that if I didn't walk through the door that night, it might never open for me again.

*I'd better take this while it's here.*

Before, my heart had seemed calloused. Now it felt soft and raw and was completely breaking.

Right there in my seat, for the first time in my life, I was finally getting what the gospel was about. I realized that all the sin in my life was just like Naaman's leprosy, and the reckless lifestyle I had been living was decaying me.

But I also realized that if I got humble before God, he could instantly and completely forgive me for all the horrible things I had done. God could do for my life what he had done for Naaman's skin. I believed I could be given a new start through God.

*My life could be like that baby's skin.*

Wow! That mental picture blew me away.

Still in my seat, I started telling God how sorry I was for all the things I had done wrong. I told him I wanted to put my faith and trust in him.

I looked up to the platform.

"Those whom Jesus calls, he calls openly and publicly," Pastor Laurie said. He quoted Matthew 10:32-33: "Whoever acknowledges me before others, I will also acknowledge before my Father in heaven. But whoever disowns me before others, I will disown before my Father in heaven" (NIV).

At that point, Pastor Laurie bowed his head and began to pray. People all across the tent were praying. *I* was praying. When Pastor Laurie concluded his prayer, he looked up to face us. "If you really want to make this commitment real," he said, "raise your hand."

It happened just like I'd told Aubrey it would. But I wasn't trying to see through his words any longer.

Like many others around that tent, I raised my hand.

"If you raised your hand," Pastor Laurie continued, "stand up . . ."

I quickly stood and immediately was hit by what felt like a radical transformation taking place within me. I struggle to adequately describe what the feeling was like. But I still remember the day in 2004 when I watched on television as Scott's body was being mutilated. That day, it felt like evil was being injected into me. But on this night—March 14, 2007—I felt like *God's love* was being injected into me.

". . . and walk on forward," Pastor Laurie concluded.

Our seats were toward the back corner, so I could see people from all across the tent beginning to walk forward. I hesitated momentarily. All I could think was, *Wow! Wow! Wow!*

Before I had even taken a step toward the front, I already knew I was on a countdown clock as a Navy SEAL.

What had been my life's mission—what had consumed me through those two-plus years of training with Scott, on my own, and in BUD/S—had been replaced.

*I'm going to do what that guy up there on the stage is doing.*

That is a thought I would never have created on my own.

Up until that point, I couldn't even imagine being a regular churchgoer. As for actually getting up in front of others and talking about becoming a Christian? No way. Wouldn't happen.

And yet I knew that's what I was supposed to do.

I turned to Aubrey on my right. I'm sure I looked wild-eyed and scary to her, especially after telling her not to raise her hand after the sermon.

"Come with me," I urged her.

"No!" she told me with a you-must-be-crazy look.

So I walked to the front alone.

I had already felt a complete transformation inside of me, but when I started down the aisle, I experienced yet another new feeling: humility. That walk was like a walk of humiliation. I felt exposed, like Naaman must have felt. And I felt like a quitter—but the good kind of quitter. I was admitting that I couldn't keep living my life on my own. I was ringing the bell on my way of doing things and enlisting to live life God's way.

Such an attitude doesn't come naturally to a SEAL, who typically possesses an "I can do it all on my own" mind-set. It was a big step into humility for me to remove my trust in myself and place it completely in God. Nothing in my life—not even Hell Week—had made me feel weak. But that night I did feel weak. It wasn't what I would have thought weakness would feel like, though. Because, as I would later read in what the apostle Paul had written, in my weakness I felt God's strength.[2]

When all of us who had raised our hands had gathered in a room, we were encouraged to start reading the Bible, beginning with the Gospel of John, and to keep reading from there. The counselors also said we should let others know what had happened in our lives. I couldn't wait to tell somebody.

Aubrey and my parents were waiting for me back in the make-do sanctuary.

My parents wore humongous smiles. They started introducing me to everyone they knew from their church. "This is our son. He's a Navy SEAL, and he just made a commitment to Christ tonight!"

Aubrey's face, however, wore a different expression. She looked concerned and confused, perhaps even a little scared.

When my parents had run out of friends to introduce me to, Aubrey and I stepped aside to where we were alone.

"What's going on?" she asked me. "I'm so worried right now. What's going on?"

"We're not going out tonight," I told her, thrilled.

That night was the end of partying for me. The keg wound up sitting in my parents' garage, under that blanket, for at least two years, until the day when Dad and I were moving things around in the garage and uncovered it.

"What is this?" he asked.

I laughed.

"Oh, man," I told him. "That was from the night I got saved."

# CHAPTER 11

# LIGHT AND DARK

*Even if you suffer for doing what is right, God will reward*
*you for it. So don't worry or be afraid of their threats.*

1 PETER 3:14

★ ★ ★

**BY THIS POINT,** it should not come as a surprise that once
I became a Christian, I put everything I had into my
Christianity.

The people who counseled us in that little room by the
stage on the night I accepted Christ suggested that we begin
reading the Gospel of John.

I read all twenty-one chapters in a matter of days.

Then I decided to read the entire Bible.

I had been given a New Living Translation and one of
those guides that lays out a daily plan for reading the whole
Bible over a year. I read the first day, and it didn't take long,
so I decided to read another day's worth. That went quickly

too, so I went on to the third day's reading. I wound up reading fifteen days' worth of Scripture in one day. I noticed I could read through one month from the plan in only two days, and at that pace, I could read from Genesis through Revelation in twenty-four days.

I set that as my goal, and I made it.

I didn't merely read the Bible, though. I made notes as I progressed, writing observations on just about every page of my Bible. I spent every free moment reading God's Word. I just couldn't get enough of it.

Early in my reading process, I needed to address a question that had bothered me for a long time and had become a reason (or excuse) during my rebellious years for me to discount the Bible as being untrustworthy.

Matthew's Gospel tells a story about Jesus casting demons out of two men. The Gospel of Luke contains the same story, but Luke says Jesus encountered *one* demon-possessed man known as Legion.[3] Such seeming contradictions in the Bible had been at the root of my belief that as long as I had a good heart, nothing else really mattered. I had reasoned that if the Bible couldn't be trusted, then it was perfectly acceptable for me to customize Christianity according to my feelings.

I asked my parents for help, and they pointed me toward a resource from Josh McDowell that answered my question. There was no contradiction in those two accounts of the story, I learned, but merely different accounts from the different perspectives of the two writers. Luke did not write that there was *only* one man; he just wrote about *a* man. He was intrigued by the man Legion in particular and chose to focus on him in his account. Matthew was more interested in writing about *two* men who met Jesus.

McDowell further explained the two accounts by saying that one person could witness a car accident in an intersection and, in his re-creation of the event, talk only about the car that suffered the most damage. A second person who witnessed the same accident could recount the accident from his perspective and relate how the two cars collided. Although one witness talked about observing one car and the other talked about observing two cars, their stories would not contradict each other. They would simply be complementary stories told from differing perspectives.

With that explanation in mind, I went back and compared Matthew's and Luke's passages. It all made perfect sense.

*That was easy*, I thought.

I liked Josh McDowell's explanation so much that I looked up information about him and learned that he was an intellectual who could defend the Bible using the simplest and most understandable methods. My dad kept me supplied with Josh McDowell CDs that I could listen to on my weekend trips from San Diego to home and back.

The writings of Lee Strobel also had a major influence on me, especially in my early days as a Christian. Strobel, a former atheist and journalist turned pastor and bestselling writer, is one of today's most noted Christian apologists. I soaked up the wisdom of people such as Lee Strobel, Josh McDowell, and Jon Courson, who spoke and wrote so passionately yet so reasonably in defense of the gospel. Because of them, I wanted not only to be able to share my faith with others but also to defend it.

My fellow Team 1 members knew I had become a Christian. I let them know right away, telling the first SEAL I saw after returning from the Greg Laurie crusade, "Hey, I just became a Christian."

"Okay, man," he responded. "Good for you, Williams."

I could tell he didn't take my newfound faith too seriously. Neither did any of the other SEALs at first. I understood why. Since I had joined the team, they had seen how go-with-the-flow I was with them and how willing I was to do anything they wanted me to do. I'm sure they assumed I was just going with a different flow for the moment and would soon be back in step with them.

It wouldn't be long, though, until they saw how serious I was about being a Christian—and that would cause severe problems. But first, my status as a new believer caused a problem back home in Huntington Beach.

## OFF AGAIN, BUT FOR GOOD?

I was amazed at the dramatic change that took place in my life when I put God first. I still look back in awe at the transformation that took place within me.

My arrogance disappeared, for example—perhaps because so much of my cockiness had come from my personal achievements. My sports success, my skateboarding commercials and fame, my sport-fishing gigs, my status as a Navy

SEAL trainee and then as a SEAL—they had all become my identity at various points in my life. But now that I was a Christian, my identity came from being a follower of Christ, and those things I had spent so much time, energy, and effort trying to achieve became worthless to me.

I had given all my heart to sports and skateboarding and becoming a SEAL, so those naturally became the treasures in my heart. But when I accepted Christ, he became my heart's treasure, the true center of my life. I felt so compelled to follow him and to tell others about him that I was willing to give up almost anything else in my life.

Even giving up my status as a SEAL would not have been a problem. I found that difficult to believe, but it was the truth. As for my partying ways, that was really a no-brainer for me. I suddenly had zero interest in drinking, clubbing, fighting, or getting in trouble.

There was one thing, though, that I didn't want to give up: my relationship with Aubrey.

I loved Aubrey. I had loved her for a long time, even through our breaks. I was sure she was "the one," and we had had several serious discussions along those lines. But we had been hesitant to take the next step into marriage while I was a SEAL. The SEAL lifestyle is tough on a spouse and a marriage. The long periods of separation are stressful in themselves, and the danger associated with our missions adds another layer. Knowing that every phone call or ring of the doorbell could be the one she wouldn't want to answer can take its toll on any wife.

So Aubrey and I had pretty much agreed to hold off on marriage, at least for a while, but we both assumed we'd end up together.

My becoming a Christian changed all that.

Aubrey wasn't happy with the sudden changes in my life after I got saved. In fact, they kind of freaked her out.

First there was the issue of partying. I was no longer a party boy, and I was determined not to take even one more step down that path again. I felt guilty because I was the one who had introduced Aubrey to the partying lifestyle. She was two years younger than I was, and after I turned twenty-one I frequently bought alcohol for her, my brother, and our friends. My brother was great at finding the parties, and I would get the kegs and drive everyone there. (I guess you could say he was Intelligence and I was Operations.)

But then I completely changed my lifestyle—and without notice, too—and Aubrey didn't want to change hers. More important, she didn't know how to respond to me as a new Christian. I was so fired up about my faith that it scared her. After all, I was the one who had told her not to raise her hand or anything like that after Greg Laurie spoke. Then she had watched me do everything—one step at a time—that I had told her not to "fall for." It must have seemed to her that I had drunk the Kool-Aid I told her not to drink.

Looking back, I can see that the way I acted at the time didn't help matters. I steered all our conversations toward God. I spoke in all kinds of Christian jargon that I didn't really know how to use—talking about demons and spiritual warfare. I told Aubrey several times that we were "unequally yoked" (2 Corinthians 6:14, NKJV). She had no idea what that meant, and honestly, I don't think I had a good understanding of its meaning either. That didn't stop me from using the phrase, though, and trying to explain it to her, probably about as poorly as it could be explained. My intentions were pure, but my execution was horrible.

The differences in our lifestyles and my clumsy attempts to communicate my newfound faith led to tension between Aubrey and me. The tension led to strong disagreements, even arguments. When we argued, I would tell her that our arguments were spiritual warfare. "It's the devil," I would say. And the more I talked like that, the more Aubrey came to believe, to use her words, that I had "gone psycho."

Our relationship obviously had major problems, and I worried about what might happen next.

"Take anything away from me, God, but please don't take Aubrey away from me," I kept praying. "Please convert her. Do whatever. Change her. Whatever you made me feel, please make her feel it too. But please don't take her away from me."

No matter how many times I prayed that, what I wanted to happen just wasn't happening. A month after I became a Christian, Aubrey and I parted ways. And this time we weren't just "taking a break"—we actually broke up. This time, I feared, it was for good.

## PROBLEMS ON THE TEAM

While Aubrey and I were struggling with our relationship and then calling it quits, a wedge was also developing between me and other members of my SEAL team.

At first, as I've mentioned, the news of my conversion didn't really seem to bother my fellow SEALs. I think the ones who knew how recklessly I was living believed I needed some kind of cleansing, and if that happened to come through a religious experience, so be it.

The trouble was, I had not just had a "religious experience." I had undergone a complete change of nature. And that inevitably led to problems, especially since I was a new member of the team and hadn't proved myself to them yet. It was a strange dynamic: I was supposed to be the young and impressionable one on the team, but I was no longer an empty canvas, morally speaking.

For the first couple of weeks, I had tried to share my faith with some of the others and hadn't gotten much of a response. But I wasn't going overboard trying to witness to them the way I was with Aubrey. The problems had more to do with my separating myself from the others by refusing to go out drinking or to strip clubs with them.

There were a few guys who claimed to be Christians, although I had my doubts based on their lifestyles. As I read and studied the Bible, trying to learn as much as I could, I would try to share my recent discoveries with the other self-purported believers. We would have minor disagreements—nothing at all serious—over certain points, especially ones I would bring up that didn't support the way they were living.

I started detecting a growing number of "Who do you think you are?" looks from other team members. By the time our team left for a training session in Mississippi, right on the heels of my breakup with Aubrey, their feelings had grown into an all-out resentment of me.

At our Mississippi training site, we stayed in a large, two-story house with a swimming pool and a big, unattached garage for storage. The least-experienced SEALs were expected to pick up extra duties. That's the way of life in the SEALs. So the other newer guys and I were always responsible for cleaning up after training exercises and stowing away our gear and doing all kinds of small chores like those.

One night after an all-day training exercise, a bunch of the guys decided they wanted to go out. They tried to pressure me into going to some clubs with them, but I said no. I did say, however, that I would be their designated driver and drive them to town and back to the training site afterward. I hoped that would get them off my back. At least it would ensure that someone sober drove them home.

By the time I had completed my extra duties, the first group of guys had showered and changed into civilian clothes and were ready to leave. (SEALs are allowed to go out in public in civilian clothes to avoid being recognized as SEALs.) I was just coming into the house, still wearing my green camouflage and body armor. I was sweaty and smelly from the long day of training and was desperately in need of a shower.

"Williams!" someone from the first group shouted at me as I headed upstairs. "Come on. You're driving us. Let's go!"

"Okay," I answered, "give me one minute to change."

But the guys in that group were ready to start partying and decided to leave without waiting for me.

A few minutes later the next group yelled upstairs to me, "Hey, Williams! We need a driver. On it!"

So I hustled downstairs, stepped into the driver's seat of the second group's van, and drove them to a bar. The guys knew I wouldn't drink with them, but I did go in with them. I'd been doing that because I thought it was a way of keeping up the camaraderie that is so important within a team without having to make any compromises.

As the guys became obviously drunk, I tried to distance myself from them as much as possible. There was so much tension in my gut that I didn't even order a soda to drink. And as the evening progressed, the tension got worse.

The guys kept pressuring me to drink a beer. I kept refusing. So they started trying to humiliate me in front of everyone else. Because we were in civis, the bar patrons had no idea we were SEALs. To them, we probably looked like a bunch of college guys hanging out. The others in our group were calling me names and slapping me in the face really hard as they insulted me. And other customers were looking at me as if to ask, "Are you going to take that?"

I did keep taking that. I didn't really know what else I could do because I was outnumbered five to one. Besides, when you're a new guy on a SEAL team, you can expect a certain amount of testing.

The bar closed at two thirty in the morning, and I was ready to go back to our house, but the guys wanted to go to a strip club. I had no intention of going inside the strip club with them. That was a line I would not cross. I planned to remain in our van in the parking lot until they were done in the strip club, then I could take them home and end the miserable night.

The guys didn't like that plan. They wanted me to go inside.

"Get in here with us," one said after they exited the van.

"I can't. I won't."

"What is it?"

"Well, it's a God thing," I answered.

"If you can't go do this with us," one asked, "how do we know that you could shoot? How do we know you could kill somebody when you had to? If you can't even go into just a strip club with us?"

I remained silent and behind the steering wheel.

"If you can't drink with us, how do we know that you're willing to cover our backs?"

I knew no answer would satisfy them.

"We'll cross that bridge when we get there," was all I knew to say.

That infuriated them further.

I got out of the van, but I walked the opposite direction of the strip club. I figured they wanted to go into the strip club more than they wanted to teach me a lesson at that point. I was right, because the group turned away from me and walked toward the club's front door.

Once they were inside, I returned to the van and listened to music on the radio without really knowing what was playing. I kept thinking, *This is going to stink when they come back out.*

As I thought that, Matthew 7:14 kept coming to mind: "Because narrow is the gate and difficult is the way which leads to life, and there are few who find it" (NKJV).

I knew I had chosen the narrow gate and I understood that life would be difficult at times, but this confused me. Shouldn't there have been some kind of reward for my making the best decision? And even if I wasn't actually rewarded, couldn't those guys have just been happy for me and left me alone?

Things only got worse when they returned from inside the strip club. They'd been drunk when we arrived at the club. They were even more drunk when they came back out an hour later, and they were still irritated with me for not going in with them. Once they were all in the van, I realized I'd been right. This ride really was going to stink.

When we traveled in vans, we often played what we called War Games. We would play-fight each other, throwing small punches and wrestling around. War Games had one important rule: leave the driver alone. But because the guys were wasted and rowdy and because I was a new guy, they ignored that rule. They punched me in the arm and shoulder, grabbed at me, poked at my eyes, and tried to rock the van as I drove down the road. It was more annoying than anything else, but I was relieved when we made it safely back to our training house.

*They're so drunk that they'll go to their rooms and pass out, and this whole experience will finally be over*, I thought.

They did go straight to their rooms and fall asleep, but the experience wasn't over.

It turned out that the worst was yet to come.

## RUDE AWAKENING

I went straight to my room too, and immediately fell asleep, wiped out from the long day of training and the events of the night and early morning.

The next thing I knew, I was punched hard in the stomach and pulled out of my bed and onto the floor.

The wind was knocked out of me, and I had no idea what was happening. When the bedroom light flipped on, I saw five totally drunk guys standing over me. They were guys from the first group that had wanted me to drive them the night before but had left without me because I wasn't ready.

These guys were bad news—a particularly rough group of troublemakers. In all my time in the SEALs, I never met a group as aggressive as they were. And they'd been the first to have it in for me after I became a Christian.

I could tell they didn't like being around me, and I

figured it was because they didn't feel safe talking about how they were cheating on their wives. I assumed my presence was a constant reminder to them that the things they were doing were wrong. It reminded me of what Jesus said in John 3:19-20: "Light has come into the world, and men loved darkness rather than light, because their deeds were evil. For everyone practicing evil hates the light and does not come to the light, lest his deeds should be exposed" (NKJV).

At a previous training trip in California, these guys had tried to force me to drink one night. When I wouldn't, they piled on top of me and punched me. That didn't last long, but it was enough for me to realize I didn't want to go through anything like that again.

Those guys had made it known on several occasions that they didn't want me around them anymore, and I'd been a little confused about why they singled me out to be their designated driver that night. But looking back at what happened in the hour and a half that followed that rude awakening, I think I know what they'd been planning all along.

The five guys strong-armed me and pulled me out of the room and toward the stairs. They tried to shove me down the stairs, but I grabbed onto the railing so I wouldn't fall. They kept pushing and pushing me until they had shoved me outside.

It was an unusually cold spring night in Mississippi. Temperatures had actually dropped below freezing over the previous couple of days, and we had been having cold, drizzling rain. I was wearing only gray sweatpants and a white T-shirt.

One of the guys, nicknamed Roid Rager, growled in my ear, "You think you're too good to go out with us, huh?"

His buddy, Juggernaut, grabbed me and dragged me to the corner of the pool. I could smell the alcohol still on his breath, and his speech was slurred as he cursed me.

Another guy, called Napoleon Complex, kept grabbing at me and trying to push me into the pool, but Juggernaut kept holding on to me by my T-shirt and telling Napoleon Complex, "Not yet. But don't worry, we will."

Juggernaut told me that the guys had a problem with me. They had been testing my camaraderie, and I kept refusing to do the things with them that they wanted me to do. He told me that was making them mad. Then he shoved me into the pool.

A couple of nights before, there had been a thin layer of ice on the pool's surface. The water was so cold when I first hit it that it almost took the breath out of me. Still hurting from being dragged out of the house and to the pool and now shocked by the extremely cold water, I had trouble swimming at first. I had been through a wintertime Hell Week, so I knew I could handle cold water. But during SQT in Alaska, I had been in even colder water than what we experienced during Hell Week, and I knew that in water as cold as the pool was, hypothermia can set in within minutes.

I swam toward the edge of the pool, but the guys wouldn't let me get out. They threatened to kick me in the face if I reached the edge. Then they began daring me to come to the edge so they could kick my face.

I knew better than to do that, so I started toward the shallow end, where my feet could touch the floor and I would be able to stand up. Juggernaut said that if I didn't return to the deep end, he would jump into the pool and on top of me. I went back to the deep end, but I had to fight the water to keep my head above the surface. While I struggled to tread water, the guys cursed me, called me foul names, and made it perfectly clear they hated me.

At that point, I noticed another team member, nicknamed Noble, standing by the pool. "Hey, guys," he told the others, "this is wrong." Noble, who was much closer to sober than the rest, jumped into the pool and helped me out. Juggernaut, Napoleon Complex, and another guy, nicknamed Schizo, then took me around the house to where we kept our weapons. I looked around desperately for Noble, but I couldn't see him anywhere.

The guys ordered me to take off my clothes. When I did, they started making jokes about me being naked. I was freezing, but there was no way I could escape them. Next, they forced me to do jumping jacks naked. While I did the jumping jacks, they leaned toward me and spit on me. Then they made me do push-ups, but I was so cold that I could barely extend my arms to do them.

"Stand up!" Juggernaut told me.

I did.

He stepped directly in front of my face.

"Stop shivering!"

I couldn't.

"Are you cold?!" he asked.

"Yes," I answered.

"Wrong answer!" he said, then told me to put my wet pants back on.

When my pants were on, he pulled me back to the pool and shoved me into the shallow end. "Go to the deep end and swim," he said, while still cursing me.

I went to the deep end but was unable to swim, so I worked my way back to the shallow end. At that point I didn't care if he did jump in on top of me because that sounded better than drowning.

The guys surrounded the pool and again started daring me to come to the edge and "see what happens." I basically ignored them.

Then Juggernaut issued an order I'd heard many times during BUD/S: "Duck your head underwater! One, two, three, hide the trainee!"

I did as he said the first few times he said it, then stopped because of the cold.

"Get out of the pool!" Juggernaut barked.

"Run!" the others began yelling at me when I was outside of the pool. "Hurry up! Run!"

I felt like I was trying to run on stubs. I looked down to my feet, which I couldn't feel, and saw that my ankles were basically turning over with each step.

The guys took me to the garage and ordered me to do more push-ups. I could barely lift my body off the floor.

They started spitting on me again, kicked me once, and commanded me to do jumping jacks again.

I did the jumping jacks but could tell my body lacked coordination.

The whole time, the guys continued to call me foul names. Juggernaut got back into my face, his breath reeking of alcohol, and told me again to stop shivering. Again, I couldn't.

"Are you cold?" he asked me once more.

"Yes!" I yelled to him.

"Really? Wrong answer!"

"Okay," I said, "I'm not cold!"

"Oh really?" He dragged me back over to the pool and berated me there. He kept acting like he was going to punch me, so I would flinch. Each time I flinched, he laughed.

"Are you worried I'm going to hit you?" he asked.

Before I could answer, he continued, "I'm not going to hit you because I would kill you if I started hitting you. I would smash your face. I would kill you." (That's a rough translation of what he said, minus all the f-bombs.)

Then he head-butted me.

I fell backward. I'm pretty sure the back of my head hit the concrete and I got knocked out, because the next thing I remember is being confused and dizzy and not feeling any cold at all. I was numb. But then the cold feeling returned and my senses started coming back to me.

The guys pulled me to my feet and grabbed me, and that's when Noble appeared again.

"Why did you do that?" he said to Juggernaut.

"He's faking it," Juggernaut answered. Then he shoved me back into the pool.

As I raised my head back above the surface of the water, I began fearing for my life. I didn't think I could stay in that cold water much longer without dying. I didn't care if they attacked me. I was dangerously cold and had to get out, so I headed for the edge of the pool.

When I got out of the pool, they hauled me back to the garage for more jumping jacks and push-ups and more spitting on me. Then they took me back to the pool and shoved me in again. This time Juggernaut told me the only way I could get out of the pool was to swim from the deep end to the shallow end—underwater.

I tried, but I couldn't do it. I raised my head above water and couldn't think of what else to do other than cry out, "God!" in a loud voice.

That seemed to make Juggernaut nervous.

*He won't stop unless I start making a lot of noise*, I realized.

When I started to yell again, Juggernaut ordered me out of the pool and back to the garage, where he resumed the cursing and spitting and made me do more jumping jacks and push-ups.

"We should shave his head," Juggernaut told the others. He sent the others to get a buzzer for my hair. They came back with one of the new officers, who had the buzzer. He saw me in the push-up position, saw how wet I was and how much I was shivering, but he didn't want to be the guy to intervene. He just left, and I didn't see him out there again.

Napoleon Complex told me to get on my knees and put my arms in front of me like I was praying.

"Now, start acting like you're praying to Allah."

I dropped my hands.

When I again refused to follow his orders, he began shaving my head. Part of the way through, he told me, "Start shaving your own head." As I did, I could feel some of the guys spitting on my back. I knew it was happening because their spit felt warm against my cold skin.

I had a difficult time shaving my head because of how much I was shaking.

"You missed a spot there!" one would yell at me.

"You missed a spot there, too!" another would say.

When I finished shaving my head, Juggernaut ordered me to mop up all the puddles I had left on the garage floor and clean up all the hair I had shaved off. "But go put on some dry clothes first so you'll stop dripping all over the floor."

The guys then walked out of the garage and back to the house. When I had finished cleaning the garage, I returned to my room and crawled back underneath the blanket on my bed, but I couldn't fall asleep.

The next morning I ran into Bill, our leading petty officer (LPO). An LPO is like a team captain on a football team. He outranks about 90 percent of the team but still has several rungs above him on the command ladder.

Bill noticed my unevenly shaved head and the fact that I was limping from cuts on my feet. "What's going on?" he asked.

"Oh, you know, just some new-guy stuff," I told him. "Man, I don't ever want anything like that to happen to me again."

I didn't go into any more detail. The beating was bad enough. I didn't want to risk being put through anything worse for being a rat.

After that, I hit rock bottom. I couldn't sleep at night because I didn't trust the guys around me. I had lost Aubrey, probably forever. I considered hopping into one of our transport vans, driving back home to California, and leaving the military. But I knew that wasn't a realistic option. Besides, as a Christian, I didn't think I should skip out on my duties like that.

I never expected that life would become easier just because I accepted Christ into my heart. I knew that it could even become more difficult. But I never expected things would go so far downhill so quickly. I had just become a Christian, and then I got slammed by all those things.

There was never a thought of turning away from God, even though my girlfriend and SEAL team members would have gladly welcomed me back to my old lifestyle. But I was definitely confused. And frustrated.

The only thing I knew to do was to continue to study God's Word, pray, and trust that the Lord had a plan for me amid all the chaos.

## POSSIBLE TRANSFER

Our team moved on to another training facility in Kentucky. There, I decided that I needed to talk to Bill, our LPO, about what had happened in Mississippi.

I didn't know if those guys would do anything like that again. The day after they beat me down, I saw looks of guilt on their faces. They had been so drunk that I'm not sure they remembered everything they had done to me, though they could tell by my appearance the next day that they had done something. As far as I was concerned, they were capable of acting similarly again, and that wasn't a risk I could take. Next time, they might not stop until they had killed me.

So I went to Bill. I told him that what those guys did to me was well beyond the amount of hazing that was fair game for a new SEAL, that it wasn't right, and that I wanted something to be done to prevent anything like that from happening again.

"What would you like to do about this?" Bill asked.

I'd thought about that a lot. "I'd like to be in a different task unit."

"That is pretty big," Bill said. "Are you sure you want to do it?"

I assured him I did.

"You're serious about this?"

"Yeah, I'm serious."

"This is quickly going to get out of my hands," Bill warned me, explaining that having me moved to another group within Team 1 would require going above his pay grade. It wasn't a decision he could make alone, and there would probably be an investigation into the incident. I was fine with that, but I had no idea how complicated the whole thing would get.

All the way back at Coronado on the West Coast, rumors had spread about what had taken place during our training. I heard that people were saying I was a rat and I had whined about getting hazed.

I wound up getting placed in a separate hotel during this transitional stage, and a representative of SEAL Team 1 asked for my account of the story. I shared what I had written in my record book after the hazing. Predictably, the group of guys who had roughed me up were telling a different story.

When we got back to Southern California, an agent from NCIS (Naval Criminal Investigative Service) came to interview me and the others. The agent told me he could not find anyone in the platoon to corroborate my story. He said he tended to believe what I said, but there was no evidence to back up my story. The group of guys who had beaten me up had told the agent I had been drinking by the pool, fallen in, and decided to shave my own head. They said they'd had no idea what I was doing but just helped me out.

I asked if the agent had gotten in contact with Noble, the guy who helped me out of the pool.

"Yes," the agent said, "but he won't talk."

"We're not going to pursue this any further," the agent continued. "That's it. Unless you can get somebody to confirm your story, I can't help you."

I called another new member of the team. He had told me he was a Christian, and we had talked about God and faith. But he also went out drinking and to strip clubs with other team members.

"Hey, man," I told him. "You know what happened. The NCIS agent says he's talked to everybody, and he says nobody knows anything."

"Don't ever call me again," the guy said, cutting me off. "I can't talk to you."

"Dude, don't do this!" I pleaded with him.

*Click.* He ended the call there, and I never bothered calling him again.

One night during that mess, I was reading the Bible and came across 2 Timothy 2:3: "Endure suffering along with me, as a good soldier of Christ Jesus."

I was certainly suffering. While I knew that God would not give me anything that was too much for me to endure without his help, what I was going through felt like too much. Having my reputation unfairly trashed, being isolated from my group, and having to worry about reprisals when I least expected them—all that took more of a toll on me than the worst day of Hell Week.

I looked up through the ceiling.

"Lord?" I said. "Come on!"

Eventually, the whole matter reached the attention of the SEAL Team 1 master chief. It was then arranged for me to meet with a different SEAL master chief who was going to get me plugged in and busy again at what I had been trained to do.

"Okay, Williams," he told me, "what do you want to do? What's your next step?"

"What are my options?" I asked.

"We can move you to another task unit," the master chief answered, "or we can move you to another team."

I knew that Team 7 was next in line to be deployed and soon would be leaving.

"Could I go with Team 7?" I asked.

The master chief said I could. Then he added, "This is one of the happiest days I've had all year."

"Why's that?" I asked.

"'Cause I'm putting another frogman in the fight."

*Yeah*, I thought to myself. *All of this stateside drama over here isn't going to matter once I get over to Iraq and we just start doing operations.*

# CHAPTER 12

# SEAL FOR CHRIST

*"I know the plans I have for you," declares the*
*LORD, "plans to prosper you and not to harm*
*you, plans to give you hope and a future."*

JEREMIAH 29:11, NIV

★ ★ ★

**BY THE TIME** all the paperwork had been completed and my transfer made official in May of 2007, Team 7 had been deployed. I immediately shipped overseas to join them.

But not in Iraq—in the Philippines.

I was bummed. The Philippines wasn't the big show. Iraq was.

Fortunately, the guys of Team 7 seemed indifferent about my incident in Mississippi. They had heard what had taken place—or at least some version of the story—but I didn't face many questions about the incident. The Team 7 members were much more levelheaded than most of the guys I had been around in Team 1.

Thanks to my new teammates' attitudes, I felt like I was getting a fresh start in the SEALs. That was a surprise. I'd expected that that night in Mississippi would be a constant issue. It was a big relief to be accepted on the new team right away.

Because many of my teammates are still in the SEALs and because there are still operations going on in the places where I was in the Philippines, I must leave out many details of my nearly six months there. But I can say that our team was split into a bunch of small groups and that we were there in a training and advisory role for the Philippine military.

Islam was spreading rapidly across the island chain at the time, and the Philippine military had its hands full with radical Muslims who were forming resistant forces, recruiting new converts to increase their numbers—and killing people.

When I first arrived in the Philippines, I walked past a line of caskets. They held ten people who been beheaded by the radical Muslims. But not just beheaded. The killers had cut off the victims' ears and private parts to send to the victims' families. Then they had sent text messages on the victims' own cell phones to inform the families what had happened.

The United States had not declared war in the Philippines, so we were greatly limited in what we could do there, other than train and assist the Philippine Marines. We used our intelligence equipment to help them locate key individuals, trained them in specific tactics, and basically led them all the way to the point of confronting those individuals. But there was a strict line we could not cross.

We were never to become directly involved in the captures, and if we were shot at, we were under orders only to evade, not actually fight back. All fighting was to be done by the Filipinos. They had their own SEALs, who had qualified through their own version of SEAL training, but their training wasn't as advanced as ours. We spent time teaching them some tactics that would enable them to combat the Muslim resistant forces.

Some of the not-so-riveting parts of my tour included serving as a Secret Service–type agent for the American ambassador in the Philippines. We accompanied the ambassador to speaking engagements and public appearances as she tried to cheer up the citizens there and let them know that Americans were present to support them. We dressed in suits and nice clothes for those assignments, concealing small weapons. Our job was to survey the surroundings to make sure there were no surprise shooters stationed on a nearby rooftop and no roadblocks being set up for an ambush.

During our last couple of months in the Philippines, I was part of a small group that went to Basilan Island, a place that had made the US news when the separatist group Abu Sayyaf held an American missionary couple and some other hostages for ransom. During a 2002 rescue attempt by US-trained Philippine commandos, the missionary husband was killed, though his wife was rescued. Since that time Basilan Island had become a hotbed of Abu Sayyaf activity. Four other SEALs and I teamed up with two Green Berets to lay the groundwork to overcome this separatist group that had been murdering and mutilating Filipino soldiers and citizens in an attempt to gain control.

Our task force was assigned to perform the initial legwork for setting up operation bases on that island. We built relationships with the Filipino soldiers who were stationed there and gathered information about the island so we could map out landing zones for helicopters. It wasn't the combat action I had hoped for when I signed up to become a SEAL, but it was still an important assignment.

During my time on the island, we operated out of a makeshift Philippine Marine base. It was like no other base I'd been on. The only thing that distinguished it from the rest of the jungle was some barbed wire rolled out on the ground. After spending some time on Basilan, I got to know the soldiers on the base. I always sensed they were afraid of the radical Muslims, and that upset me. They seemed reluctant to step into battle, so a lot of the training we provided had to involve motivation.

Because we were so close to the terrorists, we were always on the lookout. But the Muslim forces didn't seem interested in becoming involved with us Americans. I guess they thought we were too big of a dog to mess with. They knew that as long as they didn't poke us, we wouldn't bite. Our Humvees and other vehicles were never targeted that I knew of.

The Filipino Marines, however, were constantly getting ambushed. We had a communications room from which we connected with them while they were in the jungle, and we would hear gunshots over the radio and get eight-digit grids that told us they were being attacked only a mile and a half away. It was frustrating to know we could not become involved and that the only assistance we could give our Filipino friends was to help them retrieve their dead and wounded.

I remember once going to an ambush site soon after the ambush had taken place and kind of hoping we would come under attack. Then maybe we could finally do something that made a real difference. Other times I thought through how easy it would be for someone from our team to go out after dark with night-vision goggles. He wouldn't have had to go far at all, and it was highly unlikely the opposition would have any type of night-vision aids. With an Mk 46 machine gun that holds two hundred rounds and the potential for another eight hundred rounds strapped to his belt, just one of our SEALs could have easily taken out quite a few evil members of the Abu Sayyaf.

We wouldn't do that, though. Our orders were very specific and nonnegotiable. Besides, such a night mission would have gone against our SEAL training. SEALs are not sent out to kill people for the sake of killing them. When presented the option, we are taught to preserve life, regardless of whose life it is. If deadly force is required, we are not reluctant to use it. But all things being equal, we are trained to take people alive. Anyone who knows how to use a gun can go into a room and lay everyone down. But SEALs are trained to protect and preserve life first and foremost.

My SEAL buddies and I understood all that, but we still became frustrated with our inability to get involved in any combat. We had discussions about how one SEAL team could clean up shop on any island there. It would have been a piece of cake for us too. Give us a week, we said, and we'll have things taken care of on that island. But that wasn't what we were assigned to do.

For that reason and others, my first tour of duty was a letdown for me. I had trained to go to Iraq, and I felt like I needed to go to Iraq to find whatever closure I could with Scott's death. Instead, I spent the time advising and assisting the Filipino troops, helping them with their dead and wounded, providing them with good intelligence, and protecting the US ambassador. I'm not saying the work wasn't important; it just wasn't what I wanted to do.

Our assignment in the Philippines ended in October of 2007. We returned home to work up toward our next deployment, which would be eighteen months away.

While I was in the Philippines, though, developments had begun to take place that made me wonder whether I would still be a SEAL when Team 7's next tour came around.

## CLOSED DOOR

I had signed a six-year contract when I enlisted in the Navy and had almost two and a half years remaining when we returned from the Philippines. But the longer I served as a SEAL, the stronger my desire to be an evangelist grew.

I said that when I met up with Team 7 I hadn't faced many questions about that horrible night in Mississippi. One person who was interested, though, was my senior chief petty officer. He asked to hear my story right after I joined the team.

I gave him an overview of what had happened, and he asked what had caused the problem. I told him that I had become a Christian and that the other guys on the team resented me because I stopped drinking and going to strip clubs with them.

As I explained the situation, I could see from the senior chief's facial reactions that he was thinking while listening. When I finished, he asked, "Is this really what you want to do, to be a SEAL? Now that you've had this change?"

"To be honest with you," I replied, "I just want to finish up my time and get out. If I could find a way to get out early, I would take it."

"You know," he told me, "we might actually be able to work that out."

"Really?"

"Yeah. If it would be good for you, it would be good for the teams, because obviously you have this, well, tension with some of the other guys."

He paused, and what he had just said was still soaking into my mind when he began to speak again.

"Are you sure about this? I might be able to make it happen."

"I'm sure," I told him.

"Don't get your hopes up," he advised, "but I'll make some phone calls."

After we returned stateside, I remained in communication with the senior chief.

"It's looking more and more likely that we're going to be able to get you out of here," he told me during one conversation. "If you don't want to be here, you shouldn't have to be here. We'll get you on your way."

I had tried to hold down my hopes as much as I could, but after that conversation, I could no longer do so. All I cared about by then was being able to go and evangelize, yet I was being sent to places where I could share the gospel with only a small circle of people.

I had some success sharing my faith with the Filipino Marines who spoke English. I was able to lead several to Christ during our tour, and it was so affirming to my evangelism desires to have a Filipino show me where he had written in his journal, "I talked to Chad today and became born again." I also seemed to have an influence on some of the IT guys in our group. They were not SEALs, but they were with us in the Philippines to provide technological support, such as computer work, and to help us with intelligence.

My fellow SEALs, on the other hand, had proved a tough nut to crack. When I shared my faith with them, they'd usually be sort of agreeable and ask a question or two, but I could tell there wasn't fertile ground in their hearts. About all I could do among the SEALs was answer their questions to the best of my ability and try to demonstrate that Christianity is reasonable and not a blind faith.

What I really wanted to do was go out on the streets back home, where there were people I hadn't already had a chance to talk with and many more opportunities to share the gospel.

One day, the senior chief informed me it was 99.9 percent certain that I would be able to leave early. The necessary paperwork had made its way up the chain of command and needed one more signature.

I immediately thanked God. It was so obvious that he was opening a door for me to exit the SEALs so I could devote all my time to evangelism. The senior chief had been telling me not to let anyone—even family—know that I might be getting out early. But now, he said, I could start telling whoever I wanted.

And, boy, did I. I told all my family and friends. I told everyone I knew at my home church—Calvary Chapel in Costa Mesa, which operated the Christian high school I had finagled my way out of. I shared my story with members of the pastoral staff and told them that when I got out of the SEALs I wanted to do anything I could to help at the church—clean toilets, whatever; I didn't care. I just wanted to get involved in ministry any way I could.

With my SEAL duties apparently ending soon, the pastors began grooming me to start working at the church when I was out of the military.

Then I got a phone call.

It came early on a Saturday morning. The senior chief asked me to come to his office.

Saturdays were quiet on the SEAL portion of the base. We typically had weekends off when we were home, so most of the guys were off the base by then.

"Sit down. I've got to talk to you," the senior chief said when I entered his office.

*This could be good,* I thought. *Maybe they're letting me know it all worked out.*

"You know that one signature I said you needed?" the senior chief asked.

I nodded.

"You didn't get it. You're not getting out early. We have you for the next two years. You're ours. So you're going to work up to your deployment. That's it."

That short conversation rocked my world.

I was in complete disbelief as I stood and the senior chief dismissed me from his office. In my mind, I had a one-sided talk with God as I walked down the hallway and back up the stairs to our barracks.

*What is going on? God, you opened that door! You kicked it wide open. So why is that door closing? Was that not you who opened it?*

In the team locker room, I grabbed my belongings to head home to Huntington Beach for the weekend. The building was empty as I walked out, and only two vehicles were in the parking lot as I made my way to my truck. I felt my eyes filling up with tears.

*Come on*, I said to myself. *Don't do this. Don't cry about it.*

I looked to the sky. *God, am I not doing what you want me to do? Why? Why? Why did you open that door and then slam it right in my face?*

I didn't get any answers to my questions on the drive home.

To be completely honest, I don't think I was listening very hard.

## A STRANGER'S INSPIRATION

I had planned on doing some open-air preaching at the beach back home that day. I'd actually been doing that for a while. To explain, I need to back up in my story a little bit.

Immediately upon becoming a Christian, I felt the need to share my story with as many people as possible—not just with family and friends, but with people I didn't know. But I had no idea how to get started doing that.

Something I heard Greg Laurie say on the radio helped with that. He said that you don't have to be a great theologian to share the gospel with someone. Simply share your story, he said, and let people know what happened to you.

That is what I started doing. I would strike up a conversation with a total stranger and let him know that Huntington Beach was my hometown and that it was good to be home. That would lead to a question along the lines of "Where have you been?" Then I would let him know that I was in the military and had come home for the weekend, or whatever the occasion was.

Saying I was in the military would open up the conversation even more. Usually, the next step would be for that person to ask what I did in the military. I would say I was a Navy SEAL.

Now, SEALs do not typically go around broadcasting that they are SEALs. But in a one-on-one conversation, that was an okay thing to reveal.

When I said I was a SEAL, the person I was talking to— even if he had been mostly closed off during our conversation—would usually become noticeably more interested. I would use that interest as a springboard for talking about my faith.

I got pretty comfortable sharing one-on-one like that, but I also felt the desire to speak to groups of people, to be an evangelist. I had felt that calling from the first moments that I accepted Christ. But, again, I had no idea how to get started.

Then one day—and this was still before I left for the Philippines—I met an evangelist named Ray Comfort at my hometown beach. My parents had told me about a man who was at the beach every Saturday, standing on a box and sharing the gospel. They told me there were always people heckling him, but he'd just stand there on his box and answer all their questions. They suggested I go check out the man at the beach.

When I saw Ray, I immediately remembered him. I'd seen him there on the beach before I had become a Christian, although I had never stopped to listen to what he had to say. This time I had gone to the beach specifically to hear him.

About a hundred people had gathered around Ray's box, and I felt a huge adrenaline rush witnessing him interact with the hecklers. It was like I was watching an evangelism boxing match or football game. He would go back and forth with the hecklers, always giving a calm and reasoned response no matter how harsh or inflammatory the questions. I felt like I was watching a true professional at evangelism. (I truly believe that about Ray. God's hand is on him, and he is a strong force for skeptics to reckon with.)

Even though Ray's answers impressed me, his hecklers still annoyed me. Hearing them badger the guy got me worked up to the point that I could barely hold myself back. I wanted to step in physically, teach those guys a lesson. I wanted it so badly that my hands shook.

*I'll be the muscle here*, I was thinking. *I'll silence these guys so he can share the gospel message.* (Yes, I had become a Christian, but that didn't mean I'd lost all trust in my physical abilities.)

"Hey!" I finally interrupted one of the questioners. "Let him talk!"

Ray looked directly at me. "Excuse me, sir. He's *my* heckler. I prayed for him."

It took me a second to get that through my head: Ray Comfort had actually wanted the hecklers to be there. He had prayed for them to be there.

I wasn't sure what to make of that, so I just stood there and kept listening.

I met Ray a few weeks later at the beach, and I went back

to listen to him every Saturday I was home. He learned that I was a SEAL and asked me questions about what that was like. He also learned that I was a new Christian and that I felt strongly about sharing the gospel.

One day he asked if I had ever done any open-air preaching—just stood on a box like he did and shared the gospel. I told him no. I couldn't imagine doing that.

"You've jumped out of airplanes, right?" he asked.

"Of course," I said. He knew I'd done that many times as a SEAL.

"I've heard that open-air preaching is a lot like putting your foot outside the door of an airplane," he said.

*Yeah, right.*

"You don't think so?" he asked in response to my skeptical silence. "Then why don't you go ahead and give it a try?"

My first thought: *Oh, man, I'm in for it now.*

But I said I'd give it a try and stepped up onto the box.

Right away, I had my first heckler. (Unlike Ray, I had not prayed for that to happen.) And the heckling wasn't even about my witnessing. It was about my clothes. Someone yelled out an offensive comment about the brand of shirt I was wearing.

I froze for a moment.

*What am I doing up here?* my mind wanted to know. I didn't have an answer.

There were probably fifty sets of eyes staring at me to see how I would respond to that guy. I ignored the clothing critique and began sharing my testimony. I was nervous the entire time. When I stepped off the box afterward, I couldn't believe what I had just done. I received a lot of training from the Navy, but it had never prepared me to speak publicly.

At that point, I couldn't remember much of what I had said, and I was sure I hadn't spoken well. But about a dozen people came up to me, shook my hand, or patted me on the shoulder. They told me I had done a good job and that they appreciated me sharing my story.

That response turned out to be a onetime thing for me. I can't remember ever having that many people come up to me and say nice things after I stepped off the box. I'm grateful it happened that day, though, because all those kind words encouraged me to try speaking again sometime.

That's how I got my start. I have open-air preached more than a thousand times now. And that's what I had planned to do on the day I learned that I would not be allowed to leave the SEALs two years early.

I decided to go ahead and preach even though my mind was kind of in a fog with confusion over what had happened to that one, last signature. I gave my testimony to and shared the gospel with a small group at the beach. My parents stood off to the side where they could hear me without being in the group.

Although I would sometimes let strangers know in one-on-one conversations that I was a SEAL, I never let that be known when I spoke to groups. We were warned against revealing our identities as SEALs publicly. We were especially discouraged from posting anything on the Internet or saying something on camera about being a SEAL. If a newsperson asked to talk with us, we were supposed to decline to be interviewed. There actually was a lot of pressure to conceal our SEAL status, mostly for security reasons. Since deployed SEALs were sometimes involved in secret missions, it was best to reduce the chances that we could be recognized.

I knew if I spoke to a group at the beach and said I was a SEAL, it was possible that someone would record me on a cell phone. That video could then hit YouTube or someplace else on the Internet, and the higher-ups would be none too pleased to see a SEAL trying to Christianize people in public. So I was real careful not to let that out, and I had emphasized to Ray that he couldn't say anything about my being a SEAL either.

When I finished speaking that day, a stranger walked up to me and extended his right hand. "Hi, Chad," he said. "My name's Michael. I just want you to know that you did a really good job when you were up there today."

"Thanks," I said. But I wasn't sure I believed him, given how I felt that day.

"I just want to tell you something," he continued. "You know how Navy SEALs train to go overseas, and they practice what they will do?"

As soon as he said "Navy SEALs" a weird feeling came over me. I knew I hadn't given any indication that I was a SEAL.

"What did you just say?" I asked.

"You know how Navy SEALs practice whatever they're going to do over and over?"

"Wait," I said. "What are you talking about?"

Again he said the words: "Navy SEAL."

I just stood there staring at him.

"Anyway," he said, a little puzzled, "what I was thinking is, you need to be a Navy SEAL for Christ."

"Why did you say that?" I asked. "How did you know?"

"Know what?"

I pulled out my wallet and showed him my SEAL identification. Michael gave a small laugh.

"Did you know?" I asked him.

He didn't answer. He just looked me in the eye and said, "Chad, God has you exactly where he wants you, and you need to be preparing. Just like you prepare in your SEAL team, you need to be preparing as a Christian."

I'm sure I had a shocked look on my face.

"Well, it's been nice talking to you." Michael shook my hand once more, turned, and walked away.

I was so speechless that I didn't even say good-bye. I watched him walk down the steps of the beach. Then I turned toward my parents, who had heard the whole conversation. None of us could say anything. We just stood there, amazed.

From that point on, I never worried about why I hadn't been granted an early exit from the SEALs. I had thought God opened and shut the same door, but now I was convinced that he had me exactly where he wanted me.

God was in complete control of every aspect of my life, and that was all I needed to know.

## MY BIG PRAYER—ANSWERED!

For the preparation prior to our next tour, I was moved to a different platoon within Team 7. That was fine with me.

Granted a new perspective by Michael's words, I viewed the transfer not just as a new assignment from the Navy, but also as a new assignment from God. A different platoon meant a different group of guys with whom I could share my testimony and the gospel. I thought perhaps God could use me to reach them or at least I could plant seeds that might be watered later on by someone else.

We had eighteen months to prepare for our next assignment. We went through a lot of the same training as we had previously, but I noticed that we were improving the second time around. We also added to our skills, just as SQT had added an advanced level of training from what we had learned in BUD/S.

Ongoing training is especially crucial for SEALs because SEAL tactics are always changing. Teams that are deployed overseas collect information from the direct assaults and reconnaissance they're involved in, and that information becomes intelligence for future operations. SEAL teams back home are kept up-to-date on what deployed teams are observing, and new tactics are then developed.

For example, the enemy might become wise to our procedures for entering an enemy-occupied house, so we have to change the way we enter houses and become trained and proficient in those new methods. SEALs must remain a step ahead of the enemy because the element of surprise is one of the SEALs' greatest advantages.

During our preparation, I received an opportunity to go to Saudi Arabia for a five- or six-week assignment. Because of current situations, I can reveal even less about this assignment than about my time in the Philippines. Pretty much all I can tell about our military activity there is that we worked side by side with the Saudis' best military force. As a training device, we played a sort of capture-the-flag game in a fake village. Basically one other guy and I were able to defeat an entire Saudi platoon in that game. We sure had a good time bragging about that!

One thing I noticed about the Saudi soldiers was their deep dedication to their Islamic faith. I didn't agree with their beliefs, but I did admire their faithfulness. They made sure they prayed five times a day no matter what was taking place with our training. One time we were doing an exercise on a shooting range, and all the Saudis suddenly laid down their weapons and started praying. We American soldiers pulled out a football and started throwing it around while the Saudis prayed. One pass—I didn't throw it!—sailed right over the praying soldiers. I hoped they didn't notice.

Saudi Arabia was the first place I ever saw rain fall while the sun shone. And their drivers were pretty crazy. It seemed like there were no rules of the road. Some of the nastiest car accidents I've ever witnessed happened on Saudi highways.

But the highlight of my time in Saudi Arabia involved Aubrey.

While I was training with Team 7, Aubrey had called me out of the blue with a couple of questions: "Okay, so what happened, you know, that night?" She was asking about the night I got saved. "What was going on with you, and what were you feeling?"

I thought she might be letting me know that she was experiencing some of the same feelings I'd felt that night, but I wasn't sure. We didn't talk for several more weeks after that conversation.

I had been praying for Aubrey, as I prayed for a lot of other friends when they came to mind. But I was still convinced that Aubrey and I were finished, that we wouldn't get back together.

Then she e-mailed me while I was in Saudi Arabia. It was really good to hear from her. We began to e-mail back and forth, and we talked via Skype a few times too. We talked about many things, just catching up. But Aubrey also asked more questions about how I had felt the night of my salvation, and she even asked a few about the Bible. I gave her the best answers I could.

Immediately after I returned from Saudi Arabia, we arranged to meet at the Huntington Beach Pier. I took my Bible.

I have to tell you, it was great to see Aubrey. She was as beautiful as ever, and I felt a strange mixture of nervousness and familiarity just being near her. After all, we were together for a long time, and we knew each other pretty well. But I wasn't there to renew our relationship. I just wanted to apologize for my part in the breakup.

I told her I was sorry for being overzealous when I first became a Christian. I recognized that I had been reckless around her with my faith. I'd been so convinced that she needed to become a Christian like me that I'd scared her off. I had wanted to share with her all the amazing stuff I was learning, such as the historical reliability of the Resurrection or the New Testament arguments for God's existence in cosmology and morality.

But I had learned since then, I told her, that while such topics are important to address, they in themselves are not the gospel. It wasn't intellect that had led to my salvation, but the gospel message that Greg Laurie had shared and the Holy Spirit who had tugged at my heart. And I really wanted her to hear that message—for her sake, not mine.

Aubrey accepted my apology, and then she asked more questions. I was amazed at how I could answer her—not on my own ability, I was aware—and how I knew exactly where in the Bible to turn to show her what God's Word had to say about those issues.

After one question, Romans 3:23 came to mind, and I flipped there and showed it to her: "All have sinned and fall short of the glory of God" (NIV). I explained the condition of human beings—how every one of us sins and falls short—and what Christ did for us on the cross to rescue us from that condition.

Where before I had overwhelmed Aubrey with

apologetics, this time I trusted the power of God's Word. I trusted in the gospel, which, as Romans 1:16 says, is "the power of God to salvation" (NKJV).

As a result, we prayed together that night, and Aubrey accepted Christ as her Savior.

Leading her in that prayer was one of the happiest moments of my life. I could really feel God working in both of our lives during that conversation. At the same time I couldn't help thinking, *God, please don't take this away.*

Yeah, I know; I had prayed that before.

This time I had to add, *God, please don't let this be too good to be true.*

We got back together immediately. Aubrey began attending church regularly, and there was a noticeable change in her desire for knowledge and instruction in righteousness.

I had my Aubrey back. Well, not exactly. This was a new and different Aubrey.

And I was different too. I was growing as a Christian, learning to trust more and listen better. Looking back, though, I can see God's hand working in our breakup. Our separation gave us both time and space to think and to grow. As the Lord was sharpening me as a believer and teaching me to persevere through trials, he was also softening Aubrey's heart and bringing her to a place where she was prepared to leave old things behind and become a new person in Christ.

I had one more deployment coming up. I hoped and prayed that our relationship could make it through that test because I had one question that I really, really wanted to ask Aubrey.

# CHAPTER 13

# COVERED

*"No weapon formed against you shall prosper, and every*
*tongue which rises against you in judgment you shall*
*condemn. This is the heritage of the servants of the LORD,*
*and their righteousness is from Me," says the LORD.*

ISAIAH 54:17, NKJV

★   ★   ★

**IN MARCH OF 2009,** I received the assignment I had wanted
all along: a deployment to Iraq.

As I've mentioned, a SEAL team is broken up into smaller
groups. A team has various task units. Within task units are
platoons. Platoons get divided even further into fire teams
consisting of four men each. When the SEAL team is ready
to deploy, its component groups will often be sent to different places. Some members of our team went to Afghanistan,
Yemen, and the Philippines. My group headed to Iraq.

Much of our assignment involved capturing terrorist
leaders. Multiple sources in the field tracked known bad
guys, and they would feed us intelligence on the location of

those terrorists. Our job was to follow that information and apprehend the terrorists.

We never went out on an assignment planning to kill. Our preference was always to take the terrorists alive. Not only was that the proper method, but it also benefited the war effort because captured terrorists could become a source of great information for us. It was common to capture someone who would immediately offer or gladly accept our request for intelligence on other terrorists—in exchange for catching a break from us. Most feared for their lives, and while we had no intent to kill them, that fear gave us an advantage in negotiations.

Capturing a terrorist often led to follow-on operations. When we apprehended one in his house, he might tell us of another terrorist who lived four houses down from him. We would check with Intelligence to confirm the identity of this second potential target and take steps to make sure we weren't being led into a bad situation, and then we would execute a raid on that person's home and take him, too. Those types of missions were like a two-for-the-price-of-one special.

Another aspect of our assignment was going after weapons caches. For example, we would receive a report that bombs were hidden by a riverbank, and we would take explosive ordnance disposal (EOD) personnel with us to investigate. We would set up a security zone and dig for weapons, but more often than not those locations turned out to be what we called dry holes, without weapons.

Shortly after our tour began, we were called out of Iraq

for about a month. It made big news back home when four Somali pirates took an American ship hostage off the east coast of Africa. We were in our chow hall in Iraq when we first saw the television reports. Immediately, members of our team jokingly asked if I had brought all our dive gear.

I was our dive LPO (leading petty officer), and all dive gear was my responsibility. The guys had made fun of me back home as I loaded all our gear for the trip to Iraq. Who would need dive gear in Iraq, right?

Later that night we received a call to report to our master chief. We were told to ship out to Bahrain to prepare for a hostage rescue involving what we had witnessed on TV. A dust storm delayed our departure, so we left later than planned—with our dive gear—for Bahrain. We had blueprints of the hijacked boat and went through repeated dry runs, practicing how to take over the boat by force. We also anticipated follow-on missions that would take us from those specific pirates to the root of the problem—the mother ships from which the pirates operated.

It never happened. Because of our delay, Team 6 was called in ahead of us, and they completed the mission. By that point, the ship's captain had allowed himself to be held as a hostage so that his crew could be released. Three of the four pirates were in a lifeboat with him, one holding an AK-47 to the captain's back. With three simultaneous headshots, Team 6 snipers killed the pirates, and the captain's life was saved. The fourth pirate, who had not been in the lifeboat, was captured.

We were proud of how skillfully Team 6 completed the mission. To coordinate three simultaneous shots on an open sea accurately enough to kill the pirates before the captain could be shot—that's impressive. Of course, we were a little deflated, too. After all that time training to be SEALs, then practicing in Bahrain specifically for that rescue, naturally we would have liked to have been a part of the rescue. We were totally prepared for that assignment and extremely confident in our ability to pull it off successfully.

We thought we would be involved in follow-on operations for the rest of our deployment. But after about a month in Bahrain, orders came to return to Iraq.

## A FIGHT FOR FREEDOM

Our main task in Iraq was to work with the Iraqi Special Operations Forces (ISOF). At the beginning of the conflict there, US forces had played the lead role in cleaning up shop. In other words, our military did the job for the Iraqi forces. But by the time we arrived in Iraq, a transitional phase had begun. Now the Iraqis were taking the lead on those tasks, and we were there in more of a supportive role.

We worked with the ISOF guys, training them and teaching them how to shoot and work with us on operations. These joint operations were a cause for concern for us. As would be expected, the Iraqis weren't anywhere near our expertise level. Having them alongside us, much less responsible for completing assignments, felt almost like a liability. But the United States' goal at that time was to work our way out of Iraq by teaching the Iraqi forces how to stand on their own two feet and take care of their own business.

When we began working with the ISOF, I assumed they were all Muslims. I was wrong. Most of them spoke only Arabic, so there wasn't much direct communication between us and them. But we always had a contract interpreter with us.

I asked one interpreter, "So these guys are all Muslims, right?"

"No, Mr. Williams," he answered. "Actually, most of them are Christians."

I was really surprised to learn that.

One particular group we worked with had the reputation of being pretty tough guys and had been nicknamed the Dirty Brigade. I read in newspapers while I was there that this particular group was very aggressive and could be dangerous. I saw firsthand how hostile the Dirty Brigade members could be with their own people. I didn't really blame them, though, because it was for their own safety.

The Dirty Brigade's aggression was most evident when we were on the roads with them. Iraqi drivers knew not to get too close to military vehicles, but some seemed to test us, trying to see how close they could come. The Dirty Brigade didn't put up with that, and neither did we when we were driving in our vehicles. We had to be constantly on alert for car bombs and suicide drivers.

Sometimes, when a car came too close, the Dirty Brigade would fire their weapons. They wouldn't actually shoot at the car, but they would fire warning shots. That usually got the driver's attention, and he would either drive at a safer distance or pull off the road until we passed. The Dirty Brigade members preferred that drivers clear the roads completely. They were especially wary of oncoming traffic and would drive directly toward oncoming cars to force them to pull off to the side of the road. Or they would flash their lights or point their weapon lasers onto the cars a quarter mile or even a half mile up the road to signal that the drivers should pull over and make more room for us.

I didn't get to have much direct interaction with Iraqi citizens, largely because of the language barrier. My brother-in-law, Matt, a SEAL who married my sister Melissa, told me about one time when he and a few other SEALs were throwing a football around with some Iraqi kids. They tossed the ball to one kid, who caught it, turned, and took off running. They never saw the kid or the football again.

I'm often asked about Iraqi sentiment toward us as US military members. I saw both sides: appreciation and anti-American feelings. Sometimes Iraqis would wave and smile at us as we drove by. But then we also would encounter Iraqi citizens who would glare intently at us, as though they would love nothing more than to take us out.

I'll never forget seeing one Iraqi kid, who was probably about ten years old, holding a two-by-four on his shoulder like a rocket-propelled grenade and pretending to shoot us as we drove past him. I could only imagine what his parents had told him about Americans.

It still frustrates me today to hear someone say that we were only in Iraq to fight for oil money or that we were not there to fight for freedom. People who have not been in Iraq and other areas where we are presently involved in conflicts may find it difficult to grasp that there is real evil there. It is palpable—you can feel its presence. We were there to fight for the freedom of those who live under this blanket of oppression.

There are powerful forces in those places, forces that hate Israel and the United States. I have stood face-to-face with people who wanted to cut my head off for no other reason than that I was an American. They see America as a "satan," and they are willing to do anything to bring our country down . . . including attempting to bring that hatred into our homeland.

Sometimes I wish I could load up a plane full of people who don't believe that we were there to fight evil and take them to Iraq. I would walk them out onto a street where Americans have been killed fighting for freedom, let them sense the evil, and ask if they would have us walk away and leave this country—and ours—unprotected.

Having stood in many of those spots, I know how they would answer.

## GIVING UP THE LEAD

The equipment we worked with at first was incredible. We rode around in RG-33s, which are basically souped-up armored vehicles. RG-33s are designed to withstand the blast of an improvised explosive device (IED). IEDs are homemade bombs that are commonly used by terrorists and guerrillas, and they have been responsible for more than half of the coalition deaths in Iraq. Part of the RG's claim to fame is that no one has ever died from an IED blast while inside one.

The RG-33 also has a remote weapon system (RWS) with a .50-caliber machine gun mounted on the top. This machine gun is what I like to call a showstopper. Its rounds can pierce thick walls and still continue on their path, so it's easy to imagine what they can do to a human body.

The RWS also features a mounted camera that can see more than a mile ahead. The machine gun can be fired by remote, without someone having to expose himself through the top of the vehicle. In addition, because the machine gun is gyro-stabilized, we could use a laser to target a window on a house a thousand meters away from the protective cover of the RG-33. Without having to aim the gun itself, we could shoot with deadly accuracy.

The RWS has full 360-degree capabilities too. Operating it felt almost exactly like playing a video game. I specialized in heavy weapons, and an RWS-rigged RG-33 provided a rare combination of power and safety.

While working with the ISOFs, we stopped wearing our US military uniforms and traveling in vehicles such as the RG-33 that clearly were US-owned. Instead, we wore ISOF uniforms and traveled in old Humvees painted in ISOF colors. And rather than leading from out front, we were embedded with the Iraqi troops. We gradually let them begin taking the lead on operations and allowed them to gather the intelligence on the targeted terrorists. Eventually the Iraqis were doing all the planning and execution of operations, and we rode along just in case we were needed.

On one of my last operations as a SEAL, we were definitely needed.

We were within a couple of weeks from the end of our deployment and a return trip home. The ISOFs had intelligence on a man who was an Iraqi policeman by day and a terrorist by night. This policeman was known to have placed IEDs on the roads and was also a maker of suicide vests.

We had allowed the ISOFs to gather all the intelligence and put the entire operation together. We did run the information about the Iraqi policeman through our Intelligence to double-check what the Iraqis were telling us. Our sources confirmed that the policeman was indeed a terrorist. So we set out to capture him.

On the surface it seemed like a typical operation. Most of our operations had been completed within about ten to fifteen minutes after arriving at our target location, unless one led to a follow-on operation. That's because most of the time the terrorists were scared to death and gave up without a fight. So far we had never experienced anything more than a small wrestling match inside a house when capturing terrorists.

What we didn't know, however, was that this operation would be entirely different from all the rest. We had no idea that the Iraqis' source had set us up for an ambush.

## AMBUSHED

There were twelve Iraqis and about nine of us SEALs involved in this nighttime operation. We drove our five Humvees—not RG-33s—to the policeman's home. The trip was long enough that we had to bring extra diesel fuel so we could make it there and back.

I rode with my head poked through the roof of the Humvee, manning the .50-caliber machine gun. Along the way, I noticed road signs that pointed the way to Fallujah.

*Oh, man,* I thought, *these are some of the exact same signs that Scott saw on the night he was ambushed.*

I had tried not to think about Scott too much while I was in Iraq, but I couldn't help but think of him as I read those signs. He had probably looked at those signs, having no idea an ambush was waiting for him.

It never entered my mind, though, that *we* could possibly be ambushed. There was no reason to think we would, considering that every operation to that point had transpired so smoothly and easily. There was no sign that any danger was waiting for us. Or rather, there was no sign in our Humvee. The ISOFs had brought their source along with them in one of the other Humvees, thinking that someone who was riding along with us would never lead us into a bad situation. We later learned that this source had been tense and fidgety during the entire drive to the policeman's home.

There was nothing suspicious when we pulled up to the policeman's home—a large residence, almost a mansion—at the end of a T intersection. The guys who were going to make the raid got out of the Humvees and approached the house. I remained perched in my Humvee, my hands on the machine gun. Everything was quiet, just as it was supposed to be.

On a raid done correctly, there would be complete quiet beforehand. Then chaos would break out, but it would be a controlled chaos from our end because we had been through so many practice raids together that we knew each other's every move. The target or targets would panic at the sudden noise and, rattled, would become easy captures for us.

I watched through my night-vision goggles as some of our team members and the ISOFs made their way toward the house. Just before they reached the house, gunfire broke out from three different directions.

"We need to get out of here!" I heard over our radios. (The actual language was a bit more expressive.)

Most of those still in the Humvees tried to jump out of their vehicles to seek cover. The other Humvees were lined up along the road, and all were taking fire. We would later inspect the vehicles and see all the places where enemy fire had struck. There were even some rounds that had embedded sideways in the vehicles, apparently after being deflected by other bullets.

My Humvee had been backed up a little bit away from the others into a tree line. I quickly gauged where the gunfire was coming from. Despite the hail of bullets, I wasn't at all nervous. As part of our many months of training during our preparation for this deployment, we had taken part in simulated raids under all kinds of different scenarios. The training sessions even included simulated bullets that would sting us, and maybe make us bleed a little, when they hit. This felt just like one of those training sessions.

The enemy was firing tracer rounds. Tracers have a pyrotechnic charge in them. When the powder burns, the charge is ignited and creates a visible, burning tail. If you've watched combat on the television news and seen bullets flying through the air, those are tracer rounds. When you're in the middle of such a firefight with tracers, it looks like a scene out of *Star Wars*.

When tracer rounds are used, every fifth bullet or so will be a tracer. That allows the shooters to follow the bullets' trajectories to their targets and make necessary adjustments in their aim. The downside for the shooters is that the tracers also allow the opposite side—in this case, me and my .50-caliber machine gun—to see where the bullets are coming from.

The first rounds I saw were coming from my right. I also heard them whizzing overhead and tearing through the trees and bushes.

A bullet flying past creates a different sound than most people expect. When someone is firing a gun at a shooting range, for example, there is a big boom. But it's not like that when you're on the target side of the shooting. That big boom most people think of comes from behind the blast. But when a bullet goes past you, it sounds more like someone has taken a leather belt and snapped it to make a popping noise—except, of course, the belt isn't deadly like the bullet. In this case, it sounded like there were dozens of popping belts.

All this time, there were still guys in my Humvee trying to get out to support the others. The rounds hitting our vehicles kept them inside.

When I identified the gunfire coming from my right, I turned my .50 cal in that direction and spotted the area where the tracers were coming from. Then I opened fire. (Remember, the .50 cal can go through walls and still kill someone behind the wall.) Within seconds, the tracers stopped coming from that spot.

To the left, I saw guys jumping across the rooftop and firing toward us. I was pretty sure none of our men had made it to that roof yet, but I quickly radioed to make sure.

"Chief, we don't have anyone on the roof yet, do we?"

"Negative."

I took aim at the shooters exposed on the rooftop and smothered them with rounds. That spot also, as we say, cooled down. No more shots came from there.

That left one known threat to deal with. Our guys on the ground had tried to scramble back to their Humvees so we could hightail it out of there, but they were unable to do so. They wound up hiding behind an eroding cinder-block wall.

In our training, we are taught the distinction between concealment and cover. Cover designates something that actually protects you. Concealment is used for something that hides you but doesn't protect you. That cinder-block wall provided concealment only, so our guys were in a bad spot.

One shooter on the balcony had them pinned and was shooting at them.

"We can't make it back," came the call over the radios. "Bring the Humvees around."

My Humvee was moved to where the trapped guys could get behind it. The Humvee became cover for them.

Those guys were carrying M4s. We machine gunners often teased the team members with M4s, saying they were carrying peashooters. But now those peashooters proved really useful. What I thought was the lone remaining shooter had ducked out of sight, and the guys aimed their peashooters so that their lasers pointed to where he probably would next show himself.

I was ready. I aimed at the area the lasers had targeted. When he did show the very top of his head, the guys screamed, "Let him have it!"

I started to his right and worked my way back to where he had shown himself.

"Yeah! Get him!" I heard over the radio.

He had nowhere to go, and I let it all go until my gun jammed. The silence from my jammed gun was answered by silence from the balcony.

## A FINAL STANDOFF

"Let's go get him," the assault leader ordered over the radio. "Take the house."

The guys on the ground regathered to go clear the house. My concentration level was probably as sharp as it had ever been as I continued to scan the area—high and low—from behind my .50 cal. I knew that at any moment another shooter could pop his head up. If he caught me looking in another direction, he would probably shoot or throw a grenade down on me.

After all, my big gun had proved to be an attention-getter. I knew the guy behind that gun would be the first target. And now my Humvee was parked right at the front door to the home, in a much more vulnerable place than back near the tree line.

I still wasn't nervous, although my adrenaline was definitely flowing. It hits you almost like a drug, like an immediate addiction to the action. After all that training and all the driving around with nothing major happening, my attitude while gripping that machine gun was one of, *Come on. Somebody try me. Just try me.*

But then again, I didn't want anyone to try me with our SEALs and the ISOFs reorganizing to take the house. Those few moments of waiting, of knowing the silence could end with the decision of one determined terrorist, were extremely stressful.

When our guys finally entered the house—needless to say, the element of surprise was gone—they met resistance. I heard gunfire from deeper inside the house, followed by return fire from our guys. Over the radio, one of our guys said, "Chief, this guy is still breathing. He still has a heartbeat. I might be able to save him." After a brief pause, he spoke again. "Never mind, he's shot in the head." We later identified the dead man as the father of our target.

Our guys continued into the house and grabbed the policeman we had come for. I could hear through the radio the screams in Arabic and the crying of women inside. So much was going on at once, and the best thing for us to do was to get our target into a Humvee and get out of there before anything else could happen.

We didn't get out quick enough.

All the commotion had captured the attention of Iraqi police. They had partially blocked our path with their vehicles, and one policeman had his heavy weapon pointed at us. There was a momentary standoff as each side measured the other to see who would make the first move.

The decision was made for us to slowly roll forward. There was a slight opening between the Iraqi cars in the intersection that we could pass through. All our guys had their weapons pointed at the Iraqi police, and the police had their weapons pointed at us. Now I was a little nervous. We had all this military power that we could unload on them, but if that one officer with the heavy weapon pulled the trigger, there would not be time to respond before one of us was shot and killed.

The tension was almost visible in the night air as we slowly and carefully progressed between the police cars and past the ready-to-fire policemen until we had reached a safe enough distance that we could lower our weapons.

Our targeted man had been shot, though he was still

alive. His father was dead, along with who knows how many of his minions whom we had encountered outside the house.

We headed directly for headquarters, and I was in the group that helped carry the wounded policeman into the hospital as he moaned and groaned and complained about the angle at which we were holding him.

It was a little strange to think as we carried him down the hallway that here was a terrorist who had tried to kill us, who had most likely killed US soldiers either directly or indirectly, and now we were transporting him to a hospital so that his wounds could be treated and his life saved. There was a part of me that wanted to make him more comfortable and a part of me that wanted him to die for the deaths he had caused.

I know I'm not the only SEAL to have mixed feelings like that. It's part of what we do. If we absolutely have to, if it's required by the circumstances, we will not hesitate to use deadly force on a person. Then in the next moment, when the threat has cooled, we will try to save the same person's life.

The policeman/terrorist wound up surviving his wound, and from what I understand, we were able to obtain good intelligence from him.

Back at the base, we watched video of the ambush's aftermath that was filmed by an unmanned aircraft called a Predator. The footage showed dead bodies being placed in the backs of pickups and injured fighters being whisked away, presumably to hospitals.

"Who was that up on the Humvee that let it go with the .50 cal like that?" asked one of the team members named

Aaron, who had been among those caught on the ground and unable to scramble to cover.

"That was me," I told him.

Aaron was one of the guys who was a bit wary of me because I'm a Christian. Just one day before, he had asked me how he could trust that if we were caught in gunfire, I would have his back.

"Hmm," was all Aaron would say.

Miraculously, out of the twenty or so of us who were involved in that operation, only one of us was injured—an ISOF member who had been shot in his rear end. He was actually laughing about it. And I believe *miraculously* is the correct word, because when we surveyed the damage to our Humvees, we were amazed to find dozens and dozens of places where bullets had struck or become embedded.

One of the guys remarked, "Thanks for all your prayers, Williams."

"Williams," added another, "all that praying you've been doing paid off."

I don't know how serious those guys were. My guess is, not very. And even if they were serious, their acknowledgment of God in their lives was probably short lived.

But I definitely believe that the hand of God had been our cover. There is no other explanation for how we emerged from that ambush with nothing worse to report than a laughing Iraqi with a wounded backside.

# CHAPTER 14

# A NEW SEASON

*Anyone who belongs to Christ has become a new person. The old life is gone; a new life has begun!*

2 CORINTHIANS 5:17

★　★　★

OUR TEAM RETURNED home from Iraq in September of 2009. At that point I had only eight months remaining on my contract. I would be out of the SEALs well before Team 7's next deployment, so I knew I wouldn't be put through the preparation toward that next mission.

The Navy offered me a ninety-thousand-dollar bonus to sign a new contract, but I turned it down, saying not even a million-dollar offer could change my mind about leaving at the end of my contract.

I loved being a SEAL, and I still miss the actual job itself. After all, what wasn't to like? I got paid—and paid well—to jump out of airplanes, blow things up, combat dive, shoot guns all day, and stay in top physical shape. Yet there was a mutual feeling between the rest of the team and me that my leaving the SEALs was beneficial for all.

I never felt the animosity from Team 7 members that I had experienced with some of the guys on my previous team. The Team 7 members knew I was a Christian, and even though I had proved during our ambush in Iraq that I could pull the trigger to cover for my teammates, my leaving still seemed reasonable to them. A SEAL team is like a family, and I was the brother who was different from the rest of the family.

I believe it was as obvious to my teammates as it was to me that being a SEAL was no longer my primary mission in life. It hadn't been since the night I became a Christian and felt God calling me to be an evangelist.

My orders upon our return called for me to take on the coveted role of SEAL instructor—more precisely, an Indoc instructor. Instructors are specifically assigned for the different phases of training. I was one of the instructors who led new SEAL candidates through Indoctrination to prepare them for First Phase of BUD/S. I was also there again to test them in the fires of Hell Week.

It was almost like coming full circle as a SEAL. But I'll tell you, Hell Week is much easier when you put in an eight-hour shift, then head home until it's time to return for the next day's shift. It was weird to go home at night, slip into my comfortable bed, and think about how at that very same moment, the current class of SEAL candidates was probably in the cold ocean water trying to endure another surf torture without ringing the brass bell.

One great thing about being a Hell Week instructor was that I was able to stay in shape by running alongside the BUD/S class. I stayed on my feet as much as I could but still had available the option of riding inside one of the trucks when I wanted. And never did I have to run with that stinking boat rubbing a raw spot on the top of my head, although I did sneak my head underneath a boat a couple of times to push the students and show that I still had that drive within me.

Being home and knowing that I was home for good allowed me to get down to some serious business. There was one thing in particular that I had been wanting to tend to for several years: asking Aubrey to marry me. We had talked many times about marriage, but we didn't want to do it as long as I had another SEAL deployment in my future. We had even talked about it during my Iraq deployment, knowing that soon I would be coming home to stay. So I knew I wouldn't be able to surprise Aubrey by popping the question. That made me all the more determined to come up with an out-of-the-ordinary way to propose—something that *would* surprise her.

I had a couple of ideas that I bounced off Aubrey in a general sense to gauge what her reaction might be.

The first, to me, seemed like a good way for a SEAL to propose. I would tell her to meet me at a specific dock at a certain time, except I wouldn't be standing on the dock when she got there. Instead, I would arrive underwater thanks to a Dräger rebreather—with no air bubbles to give me away—and pop out of the water with her engagement ring.

That didn't elicit a positive response from Aubrey. When I later revealed all the details of my plan, she told me that if I had proposed that way, she would have said, "Try again!"

With the underwater idea nixed, I thought about telling her to meet me at a park. I would then parachute into the park, drop to one knee, and propose.

That idea never got off the ground either.

When we had stopped in jewelry stores to look at engagement rings, Aubrey had never liked the rings I liked. I definitely wanted her to have one that appealed to her, so we kept looking. One day in a Robbins Brothers store, she finally found one she liked. When Aubrey excused herself to go to the restroom, I chatted with the salesperson, Maria, who asked how I planned to propose.

I told her about the flawed scuba and parachuting ideas.

"It's good that you didn't do that," Maria said with a headshake.

While we talked, I told Maria how Aubrey and I had met at Disneyland. A lightbulb seemed to switch on above her head.

"Robbins Brothers has something of a relationship with Disney," Maria told me, "and sometimes we're able to get people up in the Disneyland castle. What would you think about that?"

"That would be perfect!" I told her.

A few days later, Maria left a message on my cell phone: "Chad, I have a really good opportunity for you proposing to Aubrey. You need to call me back right away. I can't tell you what it is, but just call me back."

I called her back, and she told me she'd been making some phone calls. Apparently Robbins Brothers was partnering with Disney for the premiere of the movie *When in Rome*, and Disney was looking for someone to propose to his future fiancée on the red carpet before the premiere. She thought that my being a SEAL gave me a great chance of being selected.

"Do you think you can keep this a secret?" Maria asked.

"You're talking to a Navy SEAL," I reminded her. "Of course I can keep it a secret."

Disneyland had hooked up SEAL teams with special offers and contests in the past, so it was easy for me to convince Aubrey that I had been invited, along with other SEALs, to the movie premiere. As the date approached, I told her that before the movie I would be interviewed about the ambush we had survived in Iraq and that the interview would take place on the red carpet. Later I told her there would be a lot of cameramen and photographers there to capture the SEALs' Disney experience.

Everything was perfectly believable, so Aubrey never suspected that anything more would happen.

She looked stunningly beautiful in her gorgeous black dress when I saw her for the first time that night. She looked like a movie star, and I felt like the movie star's date.

Together we drove to Hollywood's El Capitan Theatre for the premiere.

I had hidden the engagement ring box inside my left sock. As I walked Aubrey down a long staircase to the red carpet, she slipped a couple of times in her high heels. I grabbed her both times, but I could feel the ring box slipping out of my sock. It wasn't an ordinary-sized box, but a big box with a light in it that would shine on the diamond when the box was opened. It would have been easier to conceal a handgun than to hide that oversized box.

I worried that one more slip-and-grab might make the ring fall out of my pants leg and ruin the surprise. Fortunately, that didn't happen.

I had been given a specific spot in front of all the waiting cameras where I was to drop to my knee and propose. When I reached the coin that marked that place, I stepped directly on top of the coin, stopped, and bent over as if I needed to tie my shoe.

"Hang on," I said as Aubrey took a couple of steps ahead of me before turning around.

I tried to make it look like I was tying my shoe as I smoothly reached for the ring in my sock.

"Chad," Aubrey asked, "what are you doing?"

"Hey, baby," I said, with cameras flashing all around as I opened the ring box and showed it to her. I quoted a portion of Proverbs 31:10: "Who can find a virtuous wife? For her worth is far above rubies" (NKJV).

"Aubrey," I said, "will you marry me?"

Aubrey gave kind of a surprised chuckle, then said, "Yes."

I placed the ring on her finger, stood, and gave her a kiss as everyone along the red carpet cheered.

I was able to surprise Aubrey after all, and without having to scuba dive or jump out of an airplane. Eight months later, we were married.

## TIME TO MOVE

I technically began working in full-time ministry before leaving the Navy. I had more than a month of leave stored up that I took at the end of my service time. I officially left the military on May 18, 2010, but my leave time allowed me to start working in April with Ray Comfort at his Living Waters ministry.

Ray, the guy I had met through his open-air preaching at the beach, offered me a job as assistant director of a program that trained people to effectively share the gospel. People from all over the country and even other parts of the world would come to Southern California for a full day in a classroom setting and two "lab" days on the streets, putting into practice what we discussed in class.

As a Christian of three years at that time, I enjoyed sharing my experiences of open-air preaching with the students in the program. For the first time, I felt like I was making an impact in the area of evangelism to which God had called me. After I'd been there about a year, though, the classes began to dwindle, probably because of the poor economy and the cost for those who had to travel to Southern California. To keep me employed, Ray allowed me to become a video editor for his ministry.

It was in that position that I traveled to Israel. On May 2, 2011, my El Al Airlines flight landed in Tel Aviv. As most people on the plane began turning on their cell phones and checking messages and texts, one person got word that Osama bin Laden had been killed in Pakistan. The news spread rapidly throughout the cabin that the reign of terror by the al-Qaeda head had been brought to an end by members of SEAL Team 6.

I wasn't surprised. Even though the search for bin Laden had been a long and sometimes frustrating one, I'd fully expected that he would be found eventually, and I'd known it would be a SEAL team that would find him. I knew it was a significant moment back in the States and that Americans felt a "we" sense of pride in our military finally taking care of bin Laden. I felt an extra layer of "we" because of the SEALs' role in the capture.

When I first heard the news, my immediate reaction was one of wishing I had been a part of the operation and thinking how cool it would have been—even though those responsible for his death would be unidentified—to have taken part in such a vital and masterfully executed raid. But that lasted only a moment because I knew that God had placed me in the SEALs for a season, and that season had ended.

Even in my new season, though, I wondered about God's path for me. While I deeply appreciated how Ray had made it possible for me to remain employed with his ministry, my video editing duties increased steadily as my experience grew. The more I worked as an editor, the less time I had for street evangelism.

I began to sense a growing urge to leave my job at Living Waters. Aubrey, as the good wife that she is, asked whether I really believed what that feeling was telling me to do. "You'd be leaving a job that has a steady paycheck," she reminded me.

I was sure, but I also wasn't sure. I know that doesn't make sense unless you're a Christian who has been in a situation where you're confident God will lead you to the place he wants you to be, yet at the same time you're not confident you are actually "hearing" what he's leading you to do.

My moment of confirmation came during a church service. Our church had a guest speaker that weekend named Bob Coy, and to be honest I was tuning him out. Instead of listening, I was praying.

*Lord, do you want me to be at Living Waters or not? I'm pretty sure you want me to move. All right, I know you want me to move. But I need you to make that really clear to me.*

When I finished that prayer, I tuned back in to the speaker. "Where you are, God does not want you to be," he was saying. "He wants to move you."

*Whoa!* I thought. That was as powerful a moment as the day at the beach when a total stranger challenged me to "be a SEAL for Christ." And I paid attention. The first thing Monday, I resigned from Living Waters—with nothing else lined up.

I went to bed Monday night knowing I had made the

right decision, but I was still completely in the dark as to what God had next for me. The following morning, I received an e-mail about an opportunity for something I thought was a closed door. The result of that e-mail is the book you are reading now.

While beginning the process of writing this book, I volunteered some of my spare time to help out at Greg Laurie's church, Harvest Christian Fellowship, at the Orange County campus. That led to a part-time position teaching high schoolers and helping start an evangelism team in Orange County.

In this new role, I have been able to take teenagers out on the streets and guide them in sharing their faith. Our first night out, I helped one of our students lead two people to Christ. That night, nine people were saved through our evangelism team. Nine souls secured their eternity by choosing heaven over hell.

What an awesome way for an outreach to begin!

## SOME FINAL QUESTIONS

As I've related in this book, I have a history of going all in on something, then burning out and moving on to something else. So the obvious questions might be: Chad, what makes you think you won't burn out on evangelism—or even Christianity? Aren't you concerned you might wind up going back to your old partying ways?

My answer is simple: I am not the same Chad now that I was then. In 2 Corinthians 5:17 Paul wrote, "Anyone who belongs to Christ has become a new person. The old life is gone; a new life has begun!" On March 14, 2007, my old life disappeared and my new life took off.

The old Chad went full bore into youth baseball and skateboarding and Hollywood and sport fishing and partying and becoming a Navy SEAL because those were things that *he* wanted to do. As the old Chad, I went from one pursuit to another because none of them ever satisfied me. When I had achieved what I wanted to achieve, I was disappointed to discover that I hadn't reached that mountaintop I thought was in front of me.

But the real problem, I see now, was that I was chasing *my* pursuits. My accomplishments were *my* accomplishments. I thought all the things I did had a purpose behind them, but actually they didn't.

I—the new Chad—do have a purpose, a purpose God has given me. What I am doing now is not something that I chose to do. Public speaking does not come naturally to me. Even when I was a big, bad SEAL and a cocky guy, I was terrified at the thought of getting up in front of a group of people to speak. The first time I got up on that box at the beach and shared my testimony without preparation, I was not operating in my own strength. It took a *very* quick and humble prayer, in which I admitted I could not speak to those people without God providing me the necessary strength.

When those nine people gave their hearts to Christ the first night we took our evangelism team to the streets, that was not our accomplishment either, and it didn't happen because of my leadership. That night was God's accomplishment. My involvement in that group came about because of a series of steps the Holy Spirit led me to take.

My confidence no longer comes from the combination of my muscles and my mind, with God providing a supporting role. My confidence comes completely from God. I am a new person enjoying a new life of purpose.

I shudder to think of where I would be today if not for that transformation.

## GREATER LOVE . . .

On the night of March 14, 2007, under a tent outside a church, I came to a decision point in my life. What would I do with the ultimate sacrifice Christ had made for me? I chose to say yes to him that day, and my life has not been the same since.

Perhaps on this day, on this page of this book, you're facing that same decision point. May I ask you the same questions I faced: What will you do with the ultimate sacrifice that Christ has made for you? How will you respond to what he has done out of love for you?

If you're not sure what that means, let me tell you about two men who taught me a lot about sacrifice.

First, let me introduce you to Mike "Mikey" Monsoor, an American hero of the highest degree. Mikey graduated from BUD/S Class 250, just four classes ahead of mine. Early in my BUD/S training, I would see him walking around the training command center and think to myself, *Wow! There goes one of the guys who made it!*

Mikey always wore a smile on his face, and he had a reputation in the SEAL teams for working hard and never complaining—the silent, professional type of SEAL. He was also known for putting others first, paying more attention to their concerns than his own.

Mikey was given orders to report to Team 3, and his platoon was deployed to Iraq. They faced many gunfights while overseas in the Middle East. During one gunfight in Ramadi, Iraq, a member of Mikey's platoon went down wounded in the middle of a street. With total disregard for himself, Mikey left the safety of cover to run into the hail of enemy gunfire directed at his wounded teammate, grab the man down, and carry him from danger to safety.

For his selfless and heroic actions on that day, Mikey was awarded the Silver Star. But his greatest act of love for country and team was yet to come.

On September 29, 2006, in Ramadi, Mikey was on a rooftop with three other SEALs and eight Iraqi soldiers, providing an early-warning sniper overwatch for troops on ground level. Early that morning, insurgents attempted to maneuver troops on the ground, and Mikey's sniper team took action, eliminating two enemy insurgents. The enemy assault progressed, escalating to rocket-propelled grenades and small arms fire as the overwatch continued to provide cover.

Suddenly, from an unknown location, an Iraqi insurgent threw a fragment grenade into the overwatch position. The grenade struck Mikey in the chest. There was only one path of escape for the twelve men on that roof, and Mikey was the only one with quick access to that exit. Instead of taking that exit, though, he yelled, "Grenade!" and jumped on top of the grenade, smothering it with his body. The grenade exploded into his chest.

Mikey's body absorbed the brunt of the blast. Two of the other SEALs were wounded by the blast, and a fourth—who was only ten to fifteen feet from the grenade—was uninjured. All three of the wounded were evacuated to a combat outpost battalion aid station. Mikey died thirty minutes later at that aid station. The others lived.

Mark these words: "Greater love has no one than this, than to lay down one's life for his friends."[4]

Now let me point you to my mentor, Scott Helvenston. When Scott's vehicle was ambushed, he was mortally wounded, his vehicle set aflame. I watched on a television screen as the most incredible man I ever knew was dragged into the street and an angry Iraqi mob beat his lifeless body. After wrapping a rope around Scott's legs, the mob dragged this American hero through the streets of Fallujah to the Euphrates River bridge, where he was hung upside down.

We are all familiar with the expression, "Freedom isn't free," and we are intimately familiar with it when we consider that Scott paid the ultimate price for the freedoms we enjoy.

Mark these words again: "Greater love has no one than this, than to lay down one's life for his friends."

Finally, consider the Man who actually spoke those words

about "greater love." He is Jesus Christ. And he said them just before he went to the Cross.

You see, just as Mikey Monsoor absorbed the wrath of that grenade on himself so that his friends on the rooftop could live, Jesus Christ absorbed the wrath of our sin on himself so that *we* could live eternally and be free of the consequences of our sin.

And just as my friend Scott Helvenston was killed and hung from the Euphrates River bridge for the sake of our freedom, Jesus Christ hung on the cross of Calvary and died so that we could have freedom from sin.

*Greater love has no one than this, than to lay down one's life for his friends.*

You can see it in Mikey. You can see it in Scott. But what they did was nothing compared to what Christ has done for you and for me. Their heroic acts of love and sacrifice, remarkable as they truly are, pale in comparison to Jesus' greater love and sacrifice in dying for the entire world—and for you and me specifically. So let us look and reflect on the Cross to "Behold! The Lamb of God who takes away the sin of the world!"[5]

## WHAT COMES NEXT

Do you believe that what I testify to is true? Do you understand the loving, heroic sacrifice Jesus made to rescue you? Are you willing to trust your life to the only One who has the power to transform it and make you new?

If you have not received Jesus Christ as your Savior, I encourage you to do so right now.

Reflect for a moment on your life and man up to the fact that you have sinned. Acknowledge to God where you have fallen short and repent of those things. (That means being so sorry about your sins that you want to change your life.) Acknowledge that Jesus Christ died on the cross for your sins and that he was resurrected—thereby defeating the power that sin once had—so that you could be forgiven, your record could be cleared, and you could become a new person and have eternity together with him in his Kingdom. Then believe in Christ from a sincere heart and trust him to be your Lord and Savior.

The moment you do that, you have God's word on it—not my word, but God's word—that he will "remember [your] sins no more."[6] He will remove them from you "as far as the east is from the west."[7] He'll give you a whole new life and a new calling.

If you have just made this decision, let me be the first to welcome you into the ranks as "a good soldier of Christ Jesus."[8] But don't stop there. Go tell someone you know who is a Christian about the commitment you have made. This will help you just as it helped me in terms of accountability—because:

> as iron sharpens iron,
> so one person sharpens another.[9]

In Matthew 7:13-14, Jesus compares entering the Kingdom of Heaven to entering through a "narrow gate." That passage continues, "For wide is the gate and broad is the road that leads to destruction, and many enter through it. But small is the gate and narrow the road that leads to life, and only a few find it" (NIV).

As you know from my story, becoming a Christian doesn't guarantee that you will have an easier life. In fact, sometimes your life may get more difficult. There will be times when, as one of the few on the narrow path, you will feel outnumbered. You might even feel like you are being ganged up on. I tell you that not to discourage you, but to *encourage* you.

Daniel 3 tells the story of three men—Shadrach, Meshach, and Abednego—who were thrown into a fiery furnace for not marching to the same beat as those around them. When King Nebuchadnezzar looked into the furnace, much to his dismay, he saw four figures in the fire. "The form of the fourth," he said, "is like the Son of God."[10]

My friends, let's walk through the fire together. And remember, we are not alone as we do so. Jesus walks beside us in everything we go through. He promised, "I am with you always, even to the end of the age."[11]

I have been where you are right now, and I can tell you that the greatest decision I ever made was to get up from my seat under that tent and go ring the bell to say I wanted to quit trying to live my way and begin living God's way.

The reward for those who pass through that gate is

eternity with the One who loves his enemies so much that he sent his Son to willingly lay down his life and take the blast of sin for us.

The path *is* narrow, but the reward is great.

# NOTES

1. For Naaman's story, read 2 Kings 5.
2. See 2 Corinthians 12:8-10.
3. These two accounts are found in Matthew 8:28-34 and Luke 8:26-39.
4. John 15:13, NKJV
5. John 1:29, NKJV
6. Hebrews 8:12, NIV
7. Psalm 103:12, NIV
8. 2 Timothy 2:3
9. Proverbs 27:17, NIV
10. Daniel 3:25, NKJV
11. Matthew 28:20, NKJV

# ABOUT THE AUTHORS

**DAYS BEFORE CHAD WILLIAMS** was to report to military duty at Great Lakes naval base, he turned on the television and was greeted with the horrifying image of his mentor and training partner, US Navy SEAL Scott Helvenston, being brutally murdered in a premeditated ambush on the roads of Fallujah, Iraq.

The footage was forever imprinted in his mind: his hero, set ablaze and then hung upside down from the Euphrates River bridge while an Iraqi mob rejoiced on live television.

Steeled in his resolve, Chad followed in Scott's footsteps and completed the US military's most difficult training to become a Navy SEAL. One of only thirteen out of a class of 173 to make it through to graduation, Chad served his country on SEAL Teams 1 and 7 for five years, completing tours of duty in the Philippines, Saudi Arabia, Bahrain, and finally Iraq.

In 2007, after attending a Greg Laurie event at his parents' church, Chad accepted Christ and was radically transformed.

Since finishing his military career in May of 2010, Chad has used the experiences and discipline he learned while operating as a SEAL to communicate the gospel in many places, from the streets of Huntington Beach, California, to the Holy Land of Israel.

Chad, his wife, Aubrey, and their daughter, Ella, live in Huntington Beach, California.

**DAVID THOMAS** is a former sports columnist whose work has been honored nationally by the Associated Press Sports Editors and has garnered him the McClatchy Company President's Award for excellence in journalism. He is the author of *Remember Why You Play: Faith, Football, and a Season to Believe* and the cowriter of *All In: What It Takes to Be the Best* by Gene Chizik. A lifelong Texan and a graduate of the University of Texas at Arlington, he lives near Fort Worth, Texas, with his wife, Sally, and their two children, Ashlin and Tyson.

TO HAVE CHAD WILLIAMS SPEAK AT YOUR
CHURCH, SCHOOL, OR EVENT, VISIT

———— ★ ★ ★ ————

# WWW.SOLDIEROFCHRIST.ORG

———— ★ ★ ★ ————

# Love memoirs?
*Find your next great read at*
*MemoirAddict.com!*

At Memoir Addict, we find ordinary people
with extraordinary stories.

## Explore:

- updates on new releases
- additional stories from your favorite authors
- FREE first-chapter downloads
- discussion guides
- author videos and book trailers

- inspirational quotes to share on Pinterest, Twitter, and Facebook
- book reviews
- and so much more!

While you're there, check out our blog, featuring unique perspectives on memoirs from all facets of the publishing industry. From authors to acquisition directors to editors, we share our passion for storytelling. You'll get an insider's look at the craft of shaping a story into a captivating memoir.

**Are you a memoir addict?** Follow us on Twitter @MemoirAddict and on Facebook for updates on your favorite authors, free e-book promotions, contests, and more!

## Plus, visit BookClubHub.net to

- download free discussion guides
- get book club recommendations
- sign up for Tyndale's book club and e-newsletters

MemoirAddict.com:
ordinary people,
extraordinary
stories!